EMPOWERED HEARTS

Courageous Writers Connected by Words

Published by CreateSpace and in association with My Inspired Communications
Copyright ©2017 by Andrea Eygenraam & Individual Authors
Stratford, Ontario, Canada
First Edition, 2017

All Rights Reserved
No part of this book may be reproduced in any form or by any means (electronic or mechanical, including photocopying, recording or by any information storage and retrieval system), without written permission from the author(s) & My Inspired Communications, except for the inclusion of brief excerpts for review purposes and referenced as per appropriate methods, Each author holds individual copyright to their pieces, and their pieces alone, and may use their submissions only, for their own purposes how they deem fit. The book as a whole may not be copied by other means.

Disclaimer
This book is for entertainment and empowerment purposes. It is sold with the understanding that the author/publisher is not assured to deliver any kind of professional advice beyond coaching (eg. Legal, psychological) or be a substitute for professional assistance.

The publisher does not have control over and does not assume responsibility for the author or third-party websites. The publisher nor the author shall be liable for any physical, psychological, emotional, financial, or commercial damages, including but not limited to special, incidental, consequential or other damages.
Empowered Hearts may be purchased for educational, business or promotional purposes
Permission should be addressed in writing to
andreaeygenraam@gmail.com

Cover and Interior Design by:
Andrea Eygenraam, My Inspired Communications

ISBN-13: 978-1979412629
ISBN-10: 1979412626

Acknowledgements

My heartfelt gratitude goes out to each and every author in this book who had the courage to share their words, and heart, with the world. You are amazing and are the reason this book is in existence. Never stop writing!

To Lisa who helped dream up this idea at our Christmas tea 2016, and who runs her own writing groups as well helping people heal through their own creativity. Keep doing what you do, we are making a difference in the world!

To Gail, who started the program that introduced Lisa and I to this, and without which, many, many people wouldn't have been able to find their own voice, and realize they are deserving and worthy of putting their words out to the world. Thank you for introducing us to this so we were able to grow the process in our own way.

And to you reading this. Know that you, too, are worthy of sharing your words. Tap into your heart and listen to what it has to say. You'd be surprised at the answers when you can get quiet enough. And if you need help, try our free fall process with guided meditation to help you get out of your own way. It's worked for so many, and can work for you too, even if you think you're "not an author"

Empowered Hearts

SPRING – p.11
Beginnings, Childhood & Family
Learning and exploring

Home Is Where My Family Is: Cindy Bourgaize
Burning Desire: Jenny Kuspira
A Mother's Love: Cindy Bourgaize
The Little Things: Cindy Bourgaize
Free Spirit: Jenny Kuspira
Q & U: Jessica Schuler-Feng
Naked: Pamela Simmonds
Today: Jessica Schuler-Feng
Soul and Spirit: Jenny Kuspira
Chestnut: Jessica Schuler-Feng
The Window to my World: Pamela Simmonds
As I look out the window.......:Tammy Arbour
We Are Not Alone: Cindy Bourgaize
Garden Musings: Lisa D. Theodore

SUMMER – p.29
Love, Gratitude
Relationships & Connection

Connection: Elena Pastura
Bee Your Highest Nature: Suzie Nunes
Fire of Love: Susan Garand
Under the Moonlight: Diane O. Taylor
Passion: Abdulkarim Farah
Your Smile: Diane O. Taylor
Wish Upon a Star: Andrea Eygenraam
The Reuniting of Souls: Susan Garand
And the Ocean Here's Now: Suzie Nunes
As I picked up my pen...: Pamela Simmonds
Blue in the Gills: Sarah Farr
Quiet Place: Diane O. Taylor

First Step: Pamela Simmonds
Rope of Light: Diane O. Taylor

FALL – p.51
Nature, Change, Questions & Answers

The River – Reflections from Nature: Lisa D. Theodore
When I Stood at the Bottom of the Staircase: Andrea Beaver Dennis
Distance: Diane O. Taylor
Ships Passing in the Night: Jenny Kuspira
Cognitive Twist: Lisa Colbert
Coach Demon: Jenny Kuspira
Pieces of Resilience: Lisa Colbert
As the Snow Swirled Around Me: Andrea Beaver Dennis
Happy: Rebecca Lofsnes
Edit This History: Sarah Farr
DNA Style: Suzie Nunes
My Life is My Own: Heather Embree
Shedding My Skin: Suzie Nunes
As the Snow Fell Softly Around Me: Andrea Beaver Dennis
Today's Imagining: Lisa Colbert
On the Other Side of the Hill: Andrea Beaver Dennis
Windows to Our Soul: Jeff Martin
Nature Musings: Valerie Malcovich
Changes: Andrea Eygenraam

WINTER – p.77
Loss, Grief, Death & Faith

Memory Box: Jessica Schuler-Feng
The White Box: Jenny Kuspira
The Box: Pamela Simmonds
Bag of Butterflies: Jenny Kuspira
Gone: Jodi Cronyn
The Last Summer: Pamela Simmonds

Oi: Jodi Cronyn
Leaves: Elena Pastura
Mother's Day 2010: Andrea Eygenraam

FIRE – p.103
Burning Away the Pain to Rise like the Phoenix

Wild: Jessica Schuler-Feng
The Wolf Pack: Keith Withers
As the Leaves Blew: Andrea Eygenraam
Bitch You Don't Know Me: Pamela Simmonds
Silent Serpent: Lisa Colbert
By the Big Bulldog: Sarah Farr
Lyra: Lisa Colbert
Doorway: Jessica Schuler-Feng
The Holes: Andrea Eygenraam

AIR – p.117
Lifting up and Empowering

The Necessity of the Sunrise: Jenny Kuspira
Daybreak: Diane O. Taylor
Free Moon: Diane O. Taylor
Paradise: Jessica Schuler-Feng
A Seagull's Flight: Jeff Martin
Between Heaven and Earth: Andrea Beaver Dennis
A Little Speck: Jeff Martin

WATER – p.125
The Life Essence of Who We All Are

Do you know what you want?: Cindy Bourgaize
The Open Door Way: Norm Eygenraam
I AM: Cindy Bourgaize
Stone: Jeff Brush
Smell the Roses: Andrea Eygenraam

Freedom: Suzie Nunes
Just One More Thing….: Cindy Bourgaize
Seasons of Change: Lisa D. Theodore

EARTH – p.139
Grounding Us as One in Spirit & Meditation

Priceless is Our Worth: Lisa Colbert
Empowered Hearts: Andrea Eygenraam
You've Never Been Forgotten: Suzie Nunes
Selfless: Cindy Bourgaize
Footprints in Paradise: Lorraine Phillips
Cycles Cycles: Suzie Nunes
Scintilla: Elaine Hutchinson
Dropping into the Zone: Lisa D. Theodore
You Are Not Alone: Susan Garand
Fire Passion Meditation: Lisa Snow
Fire Ceremony Meditation: Lisa Snow
Self-Love Meditation: Andrea Eygenraam

Fanciful Focus

When I opened my heart, and let my creativity out
my reality shifted.
I began to see life through different eyes.
It was as if I had been viewing everything around me through a
screen and then, there it was, clarity.
It all made sense, I couldn't write my thoughts down fast enough,
the flood gates had been opened and all of the fragments and morsels
of my story streamed together and flowed from my mind onto paper.
I wrote on into the night until daybreak determined to stay in the
zone.
Some of my sentences had been locked away in my brain for years.
All that was buried, surfaced. It was magical.
All the while I had under thoughts, nagging below the surface, how
long is this going to last, how did I get here, will I know how to enter
this state again?

~ Cindy Bourgaize ~

Empowered Hearts

The flame burns bright inside me
I will not let it be extinguished
The fire in me ignites others
And together we burn away the toxins
Leaving only ashes after the embers die out
I will not fan them or try to ignite them again
I will watch them smolder and fade
I will rise with a stronger heart
Shining my light for all to see
A lighthouse guiding the way home
For any others willing to look for it
Open hearts letting in the light
Igniting each other and lifting all up
Rising higher than we ever have
Together we can light the world
One flame at a time becoming brighter
As we join together, stronger united
Love will not be conquered
It will spread like wildfyre
Community of love sharing, growing, learning
Lighting the way for all those willing
To dance in the flames

~ Andrea Eygenraam ~

SPRING

Beginnings, Childhood & Family

Learning and exploring

Home Is Where My Family Is

As I gazed out at the glistening sea and mesmerizing mountains that I had longed for and sought after with passion I realized in my heart that after one whirlwind year, it was time to go home.
Coming here was gutsy and thrilling, an act of self-love but as of late I had been feeling the cut of loneliness.
The separation from my family had proven to be too much, my heart ached for the touch of the tiny hands of my grandchildren, their giggles and squeals.
I wanted to get back to nurturing my relationships with my children, my family, up close, not from afar.
As I deeply breathed in the ocean air, I expressed my gratefulness to the Universe and smiled, you know, the kind of smile that lights up your whole being, for I knew I had grown more in this past year than I had in several years, and I was going home.

~ Cindy Bourgaize ~

Burning Desire

Hello to the mermaid, bird and gold
There is a sense of something new, something old

Overtures of brilliant orange and seductive blue
Short strokes, quick strokes all the way through

Moments captured in colours cool and hot
Drink in the passion of each little spot

Eye spy something new with each passing glance
Cheers to friends, it is time for our souls to dance.

~ Jenny Kuspira ~

A Mother's Love

When he was a boy, from time to time, he'd tell me how he would be a soldier someday. As his Mom, I assumed he was just being a boy, that he would eventually choose a safer career.
He did not, his inner compass had been set some time ago and he continued to gravitate toward a career in the Canadian military.
At first, I bucked, it frightened me to imagine the danger he would be facing and at the time Canada's presence in Afghanistan weighed heavily on my heart.
He, my first born, I, a single parent, I hadn't been supporting his decision, until one day it occurred to me that it was not my decision to make. I had raised a fine young man who was choosing to serve his country.
Difficult to surrender, I knew it was time to support my son in his choice.
It was a colorful sunny fall day, we loaded the car with his things, the car ride was uneasy, we joked a bit, nervously, both uncertain about what the future had in store.
As we pulled into the train station, I fought hard to keep my emotions at bay, the painful lump in my throat would rise and I would force it back down, though I squeezed my eyes tightly, trickles of tears escaped and I'd quickly wipe away the evidence. Though I felt I was dying inside, I wanted him to leave for basic training not worrying about how broken I was.
As he boarded the train that day I felt a tinge of jealousy, jealousy toward the Canadian Army, they were gaining my son, my boy.
As I watched the train pull away from the station that day I waved and gestured that my heart was with him, all the while a thought echoed in my mind, "He would be a part of a new family now", and with that came the release of all of my held back emotions, I sat in my car alone and bawled.

~ Cindy Bourgaize ~

The Little Things

As I picked up my pen to write something meaningful today, I began to gaze about the room when I spotted a goldfish cracker under the corner of my sofa.
I smiled lovingly and was grateful for the wee reminder of my overnight guests this past weekend, my two very active and adorable grandsons.
My first instinct was to grab it and put it in the garbage, but then I thought, why pick it up? Just leave it there and enjoy the sensation of love that wells up inside my chest each time it catches my eye and savour the memories it invokes of the cherished moments of just hanging out, snuggled up together, sharing snacks and peering at the well-worn books that each could recite by heart but always are the first to be chosen.
As I sit and reflect on days gone by, a single parent raising my two boys, I truly appreciate the significance of each fleeting moment and am thankful to experience this chance at being a grand-mother.

~ Cindy Bourgaize ~

Free Spirit

Don't you dare pass me by. I am passion. I am youth. I am beauty. I am a Jamaican girl.
I AM A FREE SPIRIT

My world is this canvas, my body the paint-etching out my silhouette and features through the eyes of Israel.
I AM A FREE SPIRIT

Drink in the yellow on my bare shoulder. Watch the green dance across my chest. Follow the red from my cheek to my neck.
I AM A FREE SPIRIT

My story rests between my closed eyes and my mouth. The images are hidden inside for me to see and you to feel. My eyes and mouth are the silent and secret path to my family.
I AM A FREE SPIRIT

My vision and breath unite me and my family in song, dance and celebration. Look at me and hear the message in the stillness and the silence, listen to the colours --- "spirit cannot be contained"
I AM A FREE SPIRIT

I am a Jamaican girl, I am beauty. I am youth. I am passion.
I AM A FREE SPIRIT

~ Jenny Kuspira ~

Q & U

I don't know if you're the u that this q Scrabble piece has always been looking for

I don't know if you're the song I just can't get out of my head. Or the real lyrics to the song I just can't get right

I don't think you're the night light I use to scare away the monsters in my closet, or the blankets I pull over my head to protect me from them

I don't think you're the sticks that hold up my blanket fort. And I think you might die in the fire if we played the furniture lava game

I'm not sure you could help me find Narnia. If you went in my closet you would probably only find my queerness inside

I think you might ruin the secrets of a magic trick, and find the aces hidden up the magician's sleeve

I think it was probably you who told me Santa isn't real, and the Tooth Fairy is just my parents. And I think you would've given me a quarter instead of a dollar under my pillow

I'm pretty sure it was you who made indoor recess, who made algebra pop quizzes, who invented lunch time detention

I'm pretty sure it was you who picked on my brother, who threw rocks at me on the playground, who laughed at my big teeth until I couldn't stop crying

I know you were there when Gunner died, when I found him lying on the grass motionless on his side, when Murphy could no longer use her legs, when she fell and didn't get up ever again

I know it was you who caused my parents' divorce and made them scream at each other. And you gave me the guilt I held thinking it was my fault, thinking I was no longer loved

It was you who took my innocence without my permission. And it was you who forced me not to tell anyone for another 10 years. It was you who did everything. But it's only me who can make it better again.

~ Jessica Schuler-Feng ~

Naked

In a small room
Where
All summer long
Young children
Will learn about
Insects
And butterflies
Invasive species
And birds of prey

We
Bared our souls
To one another
Naked
For four days
Sharing childhood horrors
And dead Mothers
And Sisters
Husbands and Sons
And lost loves
Disappointed Dads
And inner beauty

And how we arrived
From there to here
And here to where?

In a small room
Where
Children learn about
The beings of nature
We learned about
The nature of our beings

~ Pamela Simmonds ~

Today

Today is the first breath I draw, the first eyes I see, the first tears I cry in a world that's scary
Today is my first smile, my first giggle, my first feeling of excitement in a brand-new home
Today is the first steps I take, the first words I speak, the first time I know myself in this existence
Today is the first time I say "I love you."
Today is the first time I dance, the first time I jump, the first time I run leaving others behind me
Today is the first day I discover love of the written word, the first time I write my name, the first words I read
Today is the first time I ride a bike, the wind whipping my face, the first time I feel free
Today is my first kiss on the school playground
Today is the first time I judge myself in the mirror, the first time I'm not enough, the first time I feel ugly
Today is the first time I cry over a boy, the first time my heart breaks, the first time I struggle to be happy
Today is the first time I try pot with my friends, the first time I smoke cigarettes, the first time I get drunk
Today is the first time I make love, the first time I feel inadequate, the first time I question life
Today is the first time I know someone to die
Today is the first time I am on my own, the first time I pay bills, the first time I need to take care of myself
Today is the first time I fly in an airplane, the first time I see clouds beneath me, the first time I see the Earth itself
Today is my first time in a new country, the first time hearing a new language, the first time seeing a new culture
Today is the first time I feel beautiful, the first day I am confident in my reflection, the first time I feel strong
Today is the first time I teach, the first time I write my stories, the first time I can give back to the community
Today is the first time I find purpose in my life
Don't wait to start your Today.

~ Jessica Schuler-Feng ~

Soul and Spirit

The words my soul speaks to me say, you are fat, you are ugly, you are unworthy.
Wait a moment, that does not seem right;
let me shake my head. OK.

The words my soul speaks to me say, you are fat, you are ugly
then it becomes muffled. Thought I heard a tune, a note perhaps some music, what was that?
Let me shake my head. OK.

The words my soul speaks to me say, you are fat
Middle C peeks through, Laaaaaaaaa. I hear a whisper of a word,
WORTHY,
Let me shake my head. OK

Let me jump into the lake, deep down into the crisp cool water and return and shake my head once more. **The words of my soul speak to me say** nothing. *Silence.*

Middle C has been joined by a melody and words; you are worthy and amazing with every thought you think. Think it right or wrong this is your song. You are perfect as you are, beauty is joy, let it flow, let it flow, let it flow.

The song of my spirit lifts me beyond my own boundaries.

~ Jenny Kuspira ~

Chestnut

We are outside in my backyard. It is autumn, a beautiful crisp day. My step father is outside mowing the lawn, the whirring of the lawnmower echoing around me, the fresh scent of cut grass fills the air. A slight breeze rustles in the maple trees above me, which are already darkening to orange, rusty yellow, and crimson hues overhead. A butterfly flitters by on the wind as I absorb the scene.

My step father is a careful man. He doesn't show emotion often with hugs or "I love yous." He shows it with actions, and with always being there for me. He stops his mowing and crosses the lawn toward me and I sit, lounging under a tree with a book.
"Here, I found this for you. I know you like owls." And he returns to his work.

I look in my hand, and he had given me a beautiful little chestnut, broken in half. The inside resembles a little face of a barn owl, a hidden treasure that was revealed only once it was broken. Tears come to my eyes and this simple yet meaningful gift. I am touched.

Years after when he and my mom divorced, when he left my childhood home and drove 4 days to Alberta, I still kept the chestnut on my shelf, one of the most treasured items I ever had, next to my super grandpa statue and my sea glass. And I knew with a soft, melancholy smile, that in his own weird way, he loved me.

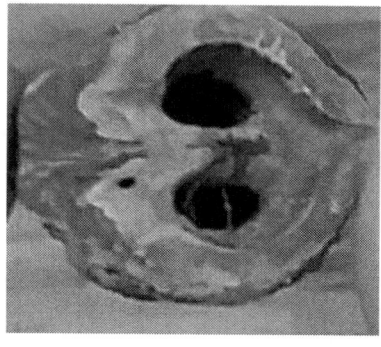

~ Jessica Schuler-Feng ~

The Window to my World

When I quietly snuck out of the house, I had no idea where I was going to go. It was 3am and they were at it again. Deep down I knew this night would go this way. Earlier I had seen the bottles on the counter and the mix in the fridge. This was what always happened when they drank. They were fun, loving parents sober, but my dad became a different person when he drank. A scary dangerous person. I could hear them screaming at each other and the sound of things being pushed about and broken in the next room. In my heart I had hoped that maybe this time they would just have a few, watch a little TV, and go to bed. Such is the naive thinking of the 15-year-old mind.

I had climbed through my bedroom window onto the ground floor patio outside our apartment. Peeking in through the sliding doors, I could see my father push my mother so violently that she hit the wall behind the couch before crumpling into a heap of legs and arms in the corner. I couldn't be sure if she was conscious. She didn't move. That scared me.

Looking back into the room I had just exited, I could see movement in the bed next to mine. My younger brother shuddered as he sobbed. I couldn't leave him here. What if our dad got tired of beating our mom? Surely, he would come in here to pick a fight with me. He'd be angry that I'd snuck out and he would take it out on this little guy instead. At 10 years old my brother was a tiny boy. Thin build and only as tall as my shoulders. Smaller than every other boy in his class, he would have been bullied except that those kids knew I would kick their asses if they did. I couldn't just leave him here to endure the rage all alone. If I was going then he was going too.

"Jimmy", I called through the window in a semi loud whisper, "Get dressed and shush. Don't let him hear you. You're coming with me." Before the sentence had left my lips, he was pushing my little chair under the window and climbing up onto the ledge. I helped him over the window track and lifted him to the ground, then pushed our bedroom window closed as quietly as I could. Grabbing him by the hand we silently walked along the sidewalk desperate to put as much distance as we could between us and the building where we lived and where the *Superintendent Office* sign hung on our door.

This little boy meant the world to me. As his big sister it had become my job to protect him from all harm, especially from the most dangerous person I knew, our own dad. We walked along in the warm summer night being careful not to be seen by passing cars. I had learned from experience that outsiders had a hard time understanding why a 15-year-old girl and a 10-year-old boy would be aimlessly walking the streets of Brampton in the middle of the night. Well-meaning citizens would call police and police would unknowingly place us right back in harm's way. Our mother, afraid of repercussions from our father, would tell them that she was ok and that it was just an argument blown out of proportion by a rebellious daughter who would use any excuse to be out past curfew. I didn't want to be out late at night. I just felt safer out there than I did in my own home. At home harm was not a possibility but a probability.

My brother and I walked around several more hours that night, hiding in the bushes along the sidewalk whenever a car approached. We headed to the playground at daybreak so we could hang out a few more hours without anyone questioning it. Nights like that were frequent that summer. Several times I had called my cousins or my boyfriend to come pick us up, but every time I did, I always felt like it was a huge burden, so eventually I stopped. Instead, my brother and I would wander around town, hiding from traffic and wait out the drunken rage. Only when I was sure my parents were sleeping it off or my father had been carted off to a drunk tank would we venture back to the apartment.

A normal teen life with best friends and sleepovers? Those things were not possible in my life. In a time when a girl should be worrying about hairstyles, clothes, and how to get the attention of that cute boy in math class, I was trying to survive maintaining grades after sleepless nights and to make it one more day without feeling the physical manifestation of my father's drunken violence. Falling asleep in school was the norm. Being made fun of by mean girls and unprofessional teachers was the norm. The experience molded me into the person I have become, but I feel that the loss of my childhood was the cost.

An excerpt from my memoir

~ Pamela Simmonds ~

As I look out the window......

I look at the sky, it is bright blue. Clouds are fluffy and soft. I am looking for the sun, I know who lives there now.
I smile through the tears and I am grateful to know where she is.
I feel pain and joy all at once, it is confusing?
I wish I could go there too someday but it is not today.

The stars have arrived. Wow, I love them so much! I could look at them all night and never get bored. I search for the dippers.
I search for the brightest. I know you are still there watching over me. You are so sparkly just like always. Oh, the glitter.... remember that?

I see the beautiful moon, it takes my breathe away. I close my eyes, breathe in deep and give my troubles, fears and sadness to it.
It continues to shine on my face and smile down on me. It gives me hope and calms my soul. I love the full moon. Thank you, God, for this eternal gift only you can give.

The window is a little foggy from my breath. I wipe it away and look back out. I see what I think is a shooting star. It is! I am so excited! I am grateful. I make a wish that I know will never come true but I am going to wish it anyway. I need God to hear it. I know you hear it.
I feel sad but grateful for all the gifts. Thank you xo

(a conversation with my Rosie)

~ Tammy Arbour ~

We Are Not Alone

Deep in the forest all alone, though she wasn't afraid; she had spent many a day playing in the forest. She loved being one with the forest.

Each tall tree stood stately, yet supporting one another as if holding hands, screening the warm rays of sunshine that trickled in to find her.

The earth's surface was spongy and light, which created an airy sense on her path toward the clearing.

An inkling of a thought brushed through her mind as she made her way, the stillness seemed unusual this day.

Though she hadn't yet reached the clearing she had already tasted the lush, juicy wild blueberries that grew there through her mind's senses.

As she stepped into the open sunlight, her heart leapt, her eyes grew wide open, she was awestruck, though too young to put a name to what she had encountered, she had discovered a group of gnomes. They quickly vanished, scattering through the trees and bushes.
She knew in her heart that they were real, that she had truly seen tiny beings and they were not a figment of her wild imagination.
She wanted so badly to share with her family what she had come upon but even at her tender age she understood that no one would believe her and that she would be dismissed, that her discovery would be viewed as nonsense.

So, she kept silent, for years, until today.

~ Cindy Bourgaize ~

Garden Musings

How inspiring it is to watch the garden grow on a warm breezy summer day. The fences are filled with morning glories crawling along the posts. Flowers are peering up to the sky leaning in to grab every ounce of sunshine available. Little red bumps starting to form into recognizable tomatoes; dark purple finger like masses dangle off the stalks of the eggplant. Birds circling all around chattering back and forth as the last of the seeds are being planted. These birds, they have radar. They know exactly when you are planting just the tastiest seeds – just for them.

Little squirrel peaks his head out of the corner of the shed. His thoughts racing away. "Wow. Look at that Giant digging in my garden! I'll just slink along the grass, dart up the tree, across the branch…Quick. Jump to the other tree before the Giant looks up. Can't be seen…. It's so exciting. I have to sing about this – oops – too loud, I've been spotted. Now what? Hurry. Flatten. The Big Ones can't see me if I am the tree. Be the Tree. Whew! Invisible again!"

Ever so deftly little squirrel scampers down the side of the enormous black walnut, under the fence, around the bushes, over the chicken wire and down…down…right into the freshly dug patch of garden. He thinks to himself, "Jackpot! The Giant left me all sorts of seeds – and if I twirl around in circles those chattery flying feathers will leave me to it! Life is so exciting!"

Robin happens to be sitting on the edge of the garden bed as little squirrel starts busting a move. He hangs out, preening himself, oblivious to the admiring stares coming his way. He bounces gently from the garden bed to the elderberry branch above and back again; like a child playing effortlessly on a trampoline. Robin would say he was more reserved than that but his Spirit tells a whole other story.

The excitement and anticipation are palpable as Robin gently waits for the next move. Ah, he spies the spy and off he goes. The tall stalks of garlic and onion provide a perfect hide and seek playground. Robin flits in and out. Stopping suddenly, he caulks his head to listen to the news on the breeze, then returns to the job at hand.

Lunch. Toddling off Robin heads to another recently hoed shady patch of dirt. Again, he stops briefly to assess the elements. Poof. Head down, beak poised. Ready...set...Lunch! A few more tasters from this garden then off Robin goes to explore the glorious world around him.

The garden rejoices in all the activity. The land is happy. The Trees are whispering to each other as they fill with winged creatures of all sorts. The beauty in the synergy of the elements comes alive in the morning sun. Oh, the adventures to be had as the garden grows.

~ Lisa D. Theodore ~

SUMMER
Love, Gratitude
Relationships & Connection

Connection

The warm sand under my feet
Always makes me feel at home.
The heat radiating up from my soles, warms my heart.
My soul sings a song of recognition
I am truly home:
At one with the earth and the sky.
My heart is full of gratitude.
The immense universe envelops me
And I float up into the warm air
The current sustains my wings…
I am home, and I have never felt happier.

~ Elena Pastura ~

Bee Your Highest Nature

In every way
And in season
From flower to flower
I search

I search
For the nectar that sustains me
The sunlight that shines in me
And in you

Round and round
Up and down
Side to side
I see

I see to trust
I see to believe
I see to learn
And I see to grow

Clear of mind
Clear of heart
I am that bee
That being clear and so free

Bee true to yourself
Bee true to me
Love is created
Into eternity

Love is a fearless state of mind
Bee that mind
In me, in you and in we
In the community

Bee simply that bee
Buzzing and tasting of life's energy
For the flow in all flowers
Are being authentic in me

In beauty and in awe
Being into self-Inspired
and boundless
In the presence of Thee

I cherish every breath
And cherish every turn
For at every moment
In present is the gift of Thee

Present and present
Step and step
Cross and cross
Together we stand

United we care
Love is what I am
Love is all there is
Love is that I am

Blessed bee we

~ Suzie Nunes ~

Fire of Love

They exchanged a glance from across the room
that sparked a fire that could not be satiated

The flames quickly spread
igniting memories of a passion they once shared
and like the smoke clouds the judgement of its victims
so did the desire that burned inside of them

Growing at a rate that was beyond control
the want for each other was irrepressible

Like the flames wrap the branches of the trees
it was only a matter of time
when their bodies would be entangled
and like the fire destroys all in it's path
each kiss diminished all the years past

The lives that had brought them to this point
would be nothing more than charred remains
and in knowing this their tears would begin to flow

Though not enough to extinguish the fire
that now burnt out of control

~ Susan Garand ~

Under the Moonlight

Smiling and laughing
like no time had passed
reminiscing about what could have been
promises unfulfilled
no expectations
no pressure
under the moonlight

Feeling special again
seeing the way you look and adore me
asking to hold me, holding *each other*
under the moonlight

Noticing that when I get close to you
it still causes a rise
awakening that spark
only you can ignite that fire within me
such magic under the moonlight

~ Diane O. Taylor ~

Passion

The depth of my soul,
I love so intensely,
and give anyone my all.

Passion fruits of labour I care,
I bare truth to the kingdom of hearts
I solemnly swear.

My kindness is repentance
For every wrong
I have ever made
And the "LOVE" I long for,
To have shared

My truth is light,
My eyes are deep.
My graces are on repeat.
Loyalty, Love, Responsibility
Are what keep me going in my reality
Despite me
Every day of the week.

Honour they better man.
So I better transcend
For I get better when I shine my light back on me
But the truth is that is
The scariest thing I have ever know.

Better to know you than me
For I am but a vessel
Of the undying devotion he gave to me

~ Abdulkarim Farah ~

Your Smile

Your Smile
Adds sunshine to my day

Your touch
Takes my fears away

Your kiss
Tells my heart to stay

~ Diane O. Taylor ~

Wish Upon a Star

The stars sparkled in the night sky
The snow twinkled on the ground, mirroring them
Sparkles above and below and the small candle in my hand warming my heart and lighting the way
The smell of rose coming from the tiny light filled the air and mingled with the winter scents of pine and hot apple cider
It was deep in the Christmas season and my heart was filled with gratitude for all that surrounded me
Carolers singing, their songs dancing on the snowflakes
Not as common anymore but thankfully on this calm night, they were there singing their love and joy, filling the ears of all who were passing by
Everything sparkled, dancing in the moonlight
Nature made their own decorations
Natural beauty trumping store bought every time
Wreaths of pine hung on the doors for the fairies
Bells ringing to let us know the angels are near
Laughter and love, as partners walk arm and arm, and kids have snow ball fights and build their new Frosty's, hopeful the other kids won't knock them down
Moving inside, out of the chill, and nearing the crackling fire, I feel cozy
The hustle and bustle of the outside world slows down inside and I'm free to cuddle under my blanket by the fire as it pops and burns
My lover heads over to me with a smile and a small surprise in his hand
He kisses my forehead and presents me with a small Christmas cracker
We pull on either end, as the toy pops loudly and explodes
With laughter, he puts on the paper crown, reading the cheesy joke
We collapse on the couch in laughter and cuddles
And I am filled with the true meaning of Christmas
Sending my wish to the star that this moment can last forever

~ Andrea Eygenraam ~

The Reuniting of Souls

Soul mates are split at the end of a life
Then search for one another in a new
Though sometimes blind to each other
A miraculous connection is made

Friendships begin, time is shared
And deep soul memories emerge
Some grow with an understanding
That their paths were meant to cross

Others with a knowing
That they complete each other's being
This feeling of wholeness
Brings confidence and certainty

Which in turn ignites a flame
That brings a glow to each other's spirits
One that shines so brightly
That those around them know

That two souls have been reunited
And God's work is not in vain

~ Susan Garand ~

And the Ocean Here's Now

CENTERING IN MY TRUE SELF
SELF COMPASSION
SELF LOVE
SELF ACCEPTANCE
INSPIRED
I BREATHE IN

INSPIRED
I AM
IN SPIRIT
HERE
NOW
UNITED
WITH YOU

IMMERSED IN YOUR DEEP WATERS
OCEAN
I AM

SWAYING
SWATHED
SOOTHED
AND HEALED
SLOWLY
GENTLY
PATIENTLY
AND
AS IT IS

URGING
ONWARD
LISTENING
LIVING WITH YOU

HEART OF OCEAN
YOU
ARE
MY BALM OF PROTECTION
ON MY SKIN
ON MY EVERY LAYER OF SKIN
INWARDS
AND
OUTWARDS
INSPIRED
IN HEART
IN SPIRIT

HERE
IS
NOW

HERE
NOW

INFINITELY BOUNDLESS
NESTLED IN YOUR DEEP
WATERS
OCEAN
I AM

HEAR
NOW

I
HEAR
YOU

F R E E

INTIMATELY BONDED
JOYOUS
ENGAGED
A CELEBRATION
A PROMISE
A COMMITMENT
TO YOU
MY BELOVED
LETTING
LOVE
BE
THE CENTER
OF MY LIFE

WE
US

UNITED AS ONE

IN GRATITUDE

IN
MY
HEART
OF HEART
THE OCEAN HERE'S NOW

~ Suzie Nunes ~

As I picked up my pen...

As I picked up my pen
The phone rang
A sister-in-law
Who didn't even notice when I put down the phone and made lunch

As I picked up my pen
The doorbell rang
The mailman
Bringing the bills that would keep my attention for hours

As I picked up my pen
The door opened
The kids
Home from school already? Where did the day go?

As I picked up my pen
The buzzer rang
The laundry
Ready to come out of the dryer and be put away before it wrinkles

As I picked up my pen
Beep... Beep...Beep
The stove timer
The casserole for dinner is ready and the family comes to the table to eat

As I picked up my pen
Mom? Mom? Mom?
My youngest
Needs help with his essay. "Please fix all my bad spelling, Mom"

As I picked up my pen
Babe...Babe...Babe
My husband
Asking me what I did all day. How come I am not spending my time with him now?

As I picked up my pen

Silence Breath Silence

Bedtime
But my mind is berating "You're not a writer. You don't even write every day"

As I drift off to sleep

Peace...Peace...Peace

I'm dreaming
Of a new day when I will pick up my pen and write

~ Pamela Simmonds ~

Blue in the Gills

You say it's just the stress of the wedding;
you can't think straight and it will be
OK
once it's all over.

You are softened by the look in his eye and the way his hand shakes
when he reads to you.

You want this to be it.
You want this relationship
cycle to stop.
You can feel it;
It's "different" somehow.
This one has sparkle and you're enamoured.

You are over-powered.

And now you're surfing the wave as it reaches closer towards shore
rising with the rhythm and purpose and tidal tilt till it
breaks into froth and white frills;
till you're blue around the gills,
and as you walk up the pathway you shrug off the chills
of what lies beneath the empty jars in the fridge.

We reach new depths when we find ourselves.

We watch, hopelessly, from the shore as others get swept away.

It works for some.

Some, who are either too stubborn to give in or actually "right" for each
other.

We place our partnerships in fickle gestures.

With infinite measure we lecture on what we want over
what we actually need; what are the realities of our
existence and how might this relate to another human
being. A good relationship is a perfect recipe.
A little of this and a little of that and a balance;
a harmonic symphony.

~ Sarah Farr ~

Quiet Place

I remember you affectionately
like a stray you brought in from the cold
feeling dreadfully lost and alone

A place that finally felt like home
with no prejudice
only support and assurance
Children playing filling the streets with laughter
Guitars strumming
drums talking
voices signing

Surrounded by big beautiful trees
walking trails and running streams
the quack of a duck, the chirp of a bird, the kuk of a squirrel
would become a sound of peace and tranquility

~ Diane O. Taylor ~

First Step

"The first step toward getting somewhere is to decide that you are not going to stay where you are."

The words glared at her from her tablet. Cody had posted the quote just an hour before announcing to her that their engagement was off. He didn't love her and he wanted to move on with the woman he did love. He had asked for the return of the engagement ring that had been his grandmother's and could she please vacate his family home by Sunday. Ashley had been devastated. Such a waste. Five years of her life down the drain. All promises of a future now residing in some stranger's bed while she sat here trying to figure out what to do with hers. The more she thought about it the more pissed off she got. All those times he was unavailable or didn't answer her texts. Each memory stoking the flames of her rage. Ashley shut down Facebook and laid the tablet on her childhood nightstand. "Asshole!" she muttered.

Nana had insisted that she pack up her important belongings and come back home right away. Pop and Jack could go back over during the weekend and get any remaining things she still had there. Then she could put Cody behind her and move on. "Easier said than done Nana", she thought. Tears flooded her eyes again as the fire of contempt burned in her veins. She had given up so much to be with Cody. A job offer that would have seen her travelling the world as a writer. Visiting little towns and reporting back to the magazine on some of the best places that were a "must see" for other travelers. But Cody had refused to let her do it, claiming that their relationship would suffer too much and that she was being selfish.
"Wasn't she happy working locally? Writing is writing right?"
And she had succumbed to his pressure and let the opportunity of a lifetime slip through her fingers. And now the relationship was over anyway.
"Fuck you, Cody" she cursed as she buried her head into her pillow and closed her eyes.

Nana and Pop were already sitting at the breakfast table when she wandered downstairs at seven. She hadn't slept well and it showed under her peacock blue eyes. Filling her plate with scrambled eggs and toast she sat across from her Pop. She peered at them quizzically as she poured herself a glass of juice. Looking like two teenagers about to get wild, their eyes sparkled and they were shifting around in their chairs. "What the heck are you two up to?" Ashley asked.

"Tell her Janice!" Pop encouraged. Nana began "Well Honey, when you were born we started putting away a little bit and we were going to give it to you next month on your birthday."
"But since you are here now, we're going to give it to you early." Pop interrupted. Ashley stared. Pop pulled the envelope from his lap where it had been hiding and slid it across the table to her. "Happy thirtieth birthday Sweetheart! Hope you like it" they chimed in together.

She picked up the large envelope and turned it over in her hands. The bold black letters of her grandparent's brokers stared back at her **CHASE AND RACINE INVESTMENTS.** Pulling the papers from the envelope she gasped as the numbers on the bottom of the page blurred together and formed a black blob.
"What?" Ashley squeaked, looking at her grandparents as they grinned back at her. "How?"

Her Pop laughed, shaking the table "Time Baby Girl, time. Put a little away, leave it alone, let the dividends reinvest and Bam". With that he pointed at the pages in her hand. As the realization of it hit her like a wet tea towel, she laughed and cried at the same time. Pages of stock codes were listed. Her grandparents had chosen stocks in companies that were relevant to her at each of her birthdays. Name brands of all the things she had consumed or loved. The portfolio had done well. Grown a little over the years and Ashley had never suspected that they had done anything like this. She hugged and kissed them both at the same time "I love you guys! I am so lucky to be the girl you raised! Thank you!"
Now she had the freedom to pursue her dreams of writing a book. At least for a year or two.

******

t behind the tiny table, her trilogy stacked around her on ike a fort. She had spent many hours perusing the shelves in this tiny shop, picking her favourites to get lost in for hours as a child and then later in high school. She loved this place and insisted that it be included on the signing tour.

The line of locals waiting to get inscribed copies extended out the door and along the sidewalk. Ashley smiled as each person congratulated her on her success and she wrote a dedication to them inside the covers of their purchases.

As the line moved along, she couldn't miss the protruding belly. "How old is this girl?" Ashley thought to herself. The young woman sat in the chair across from her. "And who would you like this dedicated to?" Ashley asked the girl who hardly looked twelve.

Panting the girl wiped the sweat from her forehead, "You can just put it to me. I'm Kallie", she answered. "I used to want to be a writer too but my husband said I should just concentrate on taking care of him, and well, now, these babies", she went on, rubbing the mass protruding from her abdomen.

Ashley's smile faded. The familiarity of the setting and the facets of the diamond catching her eye. Recognition of Cody's grandmother's ring momentarily bringing back the contempt she had felt two years ago.

"You should pursue your dream", Ashley's smile returned. Opening the cover of *Tortured Truths*, she began the dedication:
Kallie, Follow your dreams. Here is a quote that changed my life and maybe it will change yours too.
"The first step toward getting somewhere is to decide that you are not going to stay where you are."
Good luck!

And at the bottom she signed *Ashley Strong* with the tail of her g underlining her name. Her own favourite quote popped into her head as she watched the young woman fight her way back out the door.
"The best revenge is massive success" Frank Sinatra

~ Pamela Simmonds ~

Rope of Light

When the darkness comes
it takes hold of you
not willing to let go until it takes everything from you
those you care about most

You try and fight to get away
but it holds you down draining that once vibrant life out of you
others look at you and treat you differently
you don't even recognize yourself anymore
this ugly shell you have become

You're drowning struggling to break free and no one can help you
you don't *want* anyone to help you
It brings you to a place where you can't hear anyone
just the ugly words it keeps repeating to you over and over

At some point there will be a rope of light that will dangle in front of you
you may even have the strength to grab on
your hands may slip a little, but hold it tight
it's a long rope with large knots
you can see those as obstacles or
part of a ladder that helps you come out of that darkness
it's a long and difficult journey back and nothing will ever be the same

You've changed
but everyone has changed with you
and that's okay
you have built new relationships with those who have stuck by you
just hang on to that rope and let it take you to the light

~ Diane O. Taylor ~

FALL
Nature, Change, Questions & Answers

The River – Reflections from Nature

Autumn. Such a reflective time of year. A perfect season to reconnect with the pace of Nature; to harvest; to collect; to slow down. What inspirations come from connecting with the Earth; watching all the elements dancing and playing together in a rhythm all their own.

Gathering my breath, taking a long deep exhale, I begin a moment of connection – pen to paper, thought to conversation. I am listening to the inner stillness as I sit on the edge of the river wondering what stories will appear today.

Am I really listening? Am I editing – listening for a certain response? Or am I ready to loosen the grip on my mind and allow the flow of Nature to spill its story.

The words I express contain an inherent bias as they are reflections filtered through my particular perspective – The energy of the Tao, of the flow of the Universe, the Spirit that moves through all things – those words come with a different feel. It is as if my hand is connected to a different stream – just flowing forth.

Then, occasionally, there is an abrupt hesitation as the mind jumps in to second guess or examine the words that are streaming along the page. The mind has a way of stepping into our moments and creating divergences and distractions.

We talk about Flow – going with the flow – being in the flow. It's an important concept. But what does it evoke in you? What does it mean for you as part of your life?

Imagine all the rivers on the planet gently running along their path. Each drop of water has a unique role to play. The rivers themselves play a part – and that part is enriched and enhanced by all the individual participants in its path. Water droplets. Fish. Birds. Sun. Algae. Stones. Wind. Grasses. Trees. Everything that touches a drop of water in the river becomes part of the flow.

There is no disconnect. The River doesn't suddenly say, "oh, no, you swam along my shores – I am no longer a river!" She doesn't lose her identity because of the influences around her and through her. The River accepts the flow and all the magnificence that crosses her waterways.

The ducklings take their first spring bath in the tepid waters that run through the parks. Instinctively they flow – they float, they swim, they dive, they play, they eat – all along the River. Individual components creating a synergistic living environment which enhances each other's beauty.

The flow is everywhere, not just in the oceans & seas, rivers & lakes. The flow is within each of us. It is us. We are the Flow. Allowing the creative energy to course through us expands our consciousness.

Seeking the smoothness of the day, looking for our unique direction each day, sets us on a clear path. Being still, allowing the flow to flood your cells even for a moment brings your awareness to the awesomeness of YOU - the largess of Spirit that resides within and is connected with all things.

How do you know you are in the flow? How do you practice being in the flow, being the river. Checking in with our feelings – are we experiencing joy, happiness, serenity? Is there so much chaos in our world that we can't find a connection to those feelings?

Even in chaotic, hectic environments we can still embody a spirit of flow. We can embrace the unity within all things, become closer to our feelings of connection and peace. Breathing deeply. Standing at the River's edge, I allow my mind to wander, the stress and worries to float away downstream.

The River continues to flow. The moments come and go. Inspiration jumps in, motivation rises and falls.
Choose the river you want to play in today. Be the calm, clear waters reflecting back to you the vastness of Life and all the opportunities the world has to offer. Just for today, be in the flow of the river of your life!

~ Lisa D. Theodore ~

When I Stood at the Bottom of the Staircase

Empower
Abundant
Healer
Creative

How do I have to see myself on the inside to become who I want to become!

  I have to see myself as being empowered. That I have the strength to do what needs to be done. I am empowered. I have the strength and courage.
  I am abundant and I am creative. I see myself as a healer and councilor with good advice. I see myself as abundant and able to help all that need the help.

                        *   *   *

  When I stood at the bottom of the staircase I was looking up at how high and daunting it seemed to be. I know I have to climb up there, but it is so hard. How am I going to take that first step? I seem to be stuck in place. If I can just take that first step I know I can get there.
  It is just so hard. I don't know that I can do it by myself, but I am alone. There doesn't seem to be any help. There is no one there. There is no one there.
  Taking another look at the top of the stairs, I know I can do this if I can just get that foot to move just a little bit.
  It would be so much easier if I had someone to say, 'It is going to be OK'.

~ Andrea Beaver Dennis ~

Distance

we keep trying
to distance ourselves
but this merry go round
continues to lead us back into each other's arms

why don't we fight harder to walk away
you see me like no other
walking this path is a torture I choose

you know I have wings
that are beginning to spread
you too have wings
I need to let you spread
the clouds are just an inconvenient wall
that will come down

expected to move on
but everywhere I look
us
you
I know you see it too
smiling
at the thought of
unique memories unable to duplicate
you are irreplaceable
so I no longer try

~ Diane O. Taylor ~

Ships Passing in the Night

Ships passing in the night, what does it mean you ask?
"Tell me your ideas", a challenge, an interesting task.

They say that we are like ships passing in the night
Being a lady from Guelph I never considered if this was wrong or right.

The Queen Mary Two has made us strangers friendly and kind
You offer me a challenge, so this phrase sails through my mind
Traditional views of this saying suggest I think,
Of lovers or strangers who are near misses or sink
Now that I have thunk upon it a day or two
I am ready and excited to share my point of view
As a writer I often think in theme and metaphor
Perhaps the ships are about love, but I believe much, much more
Please give me some latitude and longitude if you must
I believe the ships that are passing in the night are US
Yes, in life there are near misses and direct collisions head on
But there are many things that are missed by keeping true and being strong

Life is an ocean full of swells, waves and wonder
Fear and loss make many of us cling to the rudder
Our eyes cast forward scared to look back
Searching for our destination, our home ---staying on track
Join me more deeply within my metaphor please
Think upon those emotions which make us sink or freeze
Anger, Jealousy, self-consciousness and fear
These are our pirate ships, believe me my dear, they are here.
You might think these are the strangers in the night I am suggesting
You are wrong; these are merely the ships of our testing

The ships in the night my dear friends are in our head
They are those vessels that make many of us the walking dead
I know you are clever and need no more explanation of my drift
I wish every human on the ocean of life this wee little lift
Set your sails high to catch your breeze, leave your rudder to the crew
No longer be the lost ship passing in the night, but be free and be true to you!

~ Jenny Kuspira ~

Cognitive Twist

Chasing changes or retreating in fear
Losing track of things held most dear
Living out of balance
A tight rope walk
Valuable memories sitting in hock
Look to the ring master to see what is next
A mad director keeps me hexed

Break from the state
The crazed hypnotize
Awaken the spirit and realize
Perception, reality, cognitive twist
Is that simply all that this is?
Vision coming clear, light expansion closing in
Looking for karma in my place of sin

Gaze up and see the fall wasn't that far
The key may be reached and pulled from the tar
Slowly cleaned to find release
Turning each lock toward inner peace

~ Lisa Colbert ~

Coach Demon

When **I STEPPED** forward and took the leap I fell all the way down
Cold wet pavement kissing my cheek, "who the hell are you?" my demon whispered in my ear
With a deep breath I push myself up to my knees to look and see no-one is around
"That's as good as it gets", he whispers to me, "may as well rest here my dear."

When **I JUMPED** forward and took the leap I tripped and was on my knees
Skin ripped and bloody, "I knew you would not go very far" my demon said to me sure and low
Cleaning my wound, I thought I was all alone, but then saw someone peeking through the trees
"It hurts! Rest and go home my dear. You are done, this is your best and as far as you can go."

When **I RAN** forward and took the leap I landed on my feet strong and tall
Heart racing, breathing heavy, I heard my demon yell "never again will you win this race."
Some people are waving at me and I hear them cheering, "well done, you didn't fall."
Screaming as loud as he can my demon berates me, YOU ARE OUT OF PLACE!!!

I thank you coach demon for your lessons and words of sage
I choose to fall and rise again and again and learn from your rage.

~ Jenny Kuspira ~

Pieces of Resilience

I stand to look down at myself
Viewing a figure shattered on the floor
As I reach for the pieces
I fear cutting myself more,
There are shards too sharp to add back in
Jagged corners ending, twisted edges begin
Some best left where past belongs
The segments in puzzling placement
Challenge like tiles of mah-jongg,
Some fragments so small and fragile
I fear they will be lost
The sheer project of reassembly
Brings a thought process to exhaust,
Temptation to simply sweep it up
Toss everything in trash
Turn away and run,
No stopping till next crash,
Then nothing left but sediment
Where only filth would remain
This is not an option
In it nothing but shame and pain.
Instead look back at the pieces
Find the ones that fit,

Tenacity and courage
Only segments with spirit
Faith, hope and courage
Wisdom, gratitude and grace
Each of the virtues
Will fall into their place,
When allowed to be put together
In a mosaic of light
To reflect and glint things lost
In the darkness of the night,
Day breaks again
And everything worthy is still here
Just disassembled in a disconnect
Parts polarized with fear
Slowly in a process
Where progress sometimes goes unseen
The particles will come together
With resilience in between
Authentic and with practice
Peacefully allowed
One connected masterpiece
No longer hidden
In false shroud.

~ Lisa Colbert ~

As the Snow Swirled Around Me

As the snow swirled around me I was standing in place. The cold wind touching my face. I am grateful that I remembered to put my hat, mitts and scarf on. I usually forget, sometimes on purpose. I really don't like wearing hats or mitts. I don't mind the scarves though.

I am really looking forward to spring. It brings new life, fresh scents and new sprouts. I like winter too. At least the snow. I am not too fond of the frigid temperatures. If it would stay around the 0 degree mark it would be much more pleasant and you would be able to go out and enjoy playing in it.

Can you imagine the fresh untouched snow. You gently go down and start to make snow angels. Gee I haven't done that since the kids were much younger. Or going out and making tunnels at the end of the driveway. Or making snow forts so that all the kids could have snowball fights. Oh, what fun we had when we were much younger.

Why did we stop having so much fun.

~ Andrea Beaver Dennis ~

Happy

When I look into the water in front of me I see a sadness that doesn't show in the mirror or in the eyes of others when they see me

I see a tiredness, and for a moment, I wonder, how can that be? I dip my hands into the water and splash my face with the cold wet. Maybe I didn't get enough sleep, maybe I drank too much last night or indulged in too much salty food yesterday.

I look again and it's gone, no trace of the sadness, the lethargy, but it shook me.

When I look into the water in front of me, when I look into the water in front of me, I see a drop of water make a ripple, little circles creating bigger circles rippling outward.

Is it raining? I feel the warm sun kiss my back. I glance back into the water. No trace of the drop...but then there is another. Are these tears? Why am I crying? What is so deep down and buried that I can't put my finger on it? I can't name this sadness, but it's there. It's rising to the surface, spilling out of my tear ducts, spilling out onto my page.

Happiness is no stranger to me, it is not an illusion, I know that. I know that it's an inside job and I am happy. I am happy. Aren't I?

Such a mind fuck this sadness. It's unsettling to me. Maybe it's this water? Maybe it's reminding me of something, maybe it's my own reflection, maybe it's the thoughts or the realization that everything is not as it seems.

Who knows?

Splash some more water onto my face, shake it off, it's probably nothing.

Maybe I didn't get enough sleep, maybe I drank too much last night or indulged in too much salty food yesterday.

~ Rebecca Lofsnes ~

Edit This History

When you can't undo all the hearts
for the taps and clicks
have run their course

the dance floor has emptied
and there are bottles on the floor
the temptation to unlike
deletions
edit this history
my screen
fries
fries
fries
scandalous fries

~ Sarah Farr ~

DNA Style

So today you are
Orange
In
Color
Sweet tasting
Rich in nutrients and minerals
Intense color that you are!
Increase my metabolism and help my muscles to grow
Your vitamin A heals me
Phosphorus builds, repairs, and maintains my muscles
Come into my body
And regenerate me
Come into my body
And rebuild me
As I borrow your purpose in life
You give purpose to my life
Thank you for your life
Thank you for your death
My life depends on your life
As you emerge to the best that you are
My life is enhanced
My life is nourished
My life is connected to you
Forever
We are intertwined and intimate
DNA style

~ Suzie Nunes ~

My Life is My Own

My life is my own. Today I choose to only work with people who I can get to know personally. You see, I used to believe that my emotions were too much for others. I used to keep them all inside, because nobody wants to talk about pain, fear, hurt or the realities of the suffering in our world. To actually share my truth could make others uncomfortable. Extremely uncomfortable. Because it breaks down their paradigms of how they want the world to be, or what they want to create it to be. It is their own mind trip to escape certain realities in how they, unconsciously, participate in things like sweat shop labour, or neglect or being dismissive of others, leaving a huge gap of love in the world.

I know this all too well because I grew up in a family of others who believed I was too deep or too heavy because I cared about the cruelties of the world. I had a conscience towards someone who was a complete stranger to me.

I have learned, the hard way, that people like my family can't see my heart. They had to distort it, make fun of it, demean it or be suspicious of it.

Because what I had to say didn't lend to polite or joyful conversations.

So, at different points in life, I would just stuff down my truth and feelings until I wanted to scream. I would silence myself because no one wanted to know. I so badly wanted to be loved by my family, to fit into the world in some way.

Then I realized I was creating a false sense of myself. I created my own lonely prison of niceties and pretending. This left others feeling misunderstood or unheard or abandoned, just by my lack of acknowledgment of their own humanity. Because I denied my own humanity. I perpetuated the dynamics of an uncaring world, the very thing that makes me feel ill about people.

So, I would speak up about things in little bits and pieces. And I would be abandoned, bullied and misunderstood. It got twisted and warped because, as is true to what I've learned, what I would say wouldn't be what they wanted to hear. Sure enough, it was too heavy and deep for them to get it. Or they didn't want the responsibility of having to support me in some way. But I kept speaking up anyways. You see, what I did, was I kept attracting people in my life who are like my family -- people who denied their own emotions; People who are cold or distant.

So, I've learned not to care so much about what they think. That is their journey to navigate. At this point in life, it's worse to abandon yourself than to be abandoned by others.

We all have fear and anger and hurt and sadness. This is what makes us human. This is the glue that binds us. Without these emotions, we wouldn't grow in compassion for each other.

But there are many who are terrified to admit that life isn't always wonderful. They will quickly leave or abandon someone when the going gets tough because it doesn't "feel good". They will use someone for their looks, or to help validate their own sense of self, or for even more nefarious reasons, all to add to their vision of what they want life to be.

These kinds of people scare me, quite frankly, because I know inevitably they will take something from me or hurt me. They will see me simply as a tool for their own gain, not as a person who has feelings, needs, fear and hopes.

So, this is why I make the choice to only work with people I know personally. Because I don't want to be used and disposed of, nor told that I'm too deep or too caring ever again. This is me. Take it or leave it. But I love who I am and what I care about and quite frankly we need more people like me in this world.

~ Heather Embree ~

Shedding My Skin

Shedding my skin
Shedding my skin of the old
And emerging into the new

Sometimes it hurts
But it is my choice to let go

Feeling my skin peeling
Flaking, and drying off
I wait and learn to be patient
And gentle with myself
As my old skin is dying
And my new skin is birthing

Shedding my skin
Shedding my skin of the old
And emerging into the new
I know I am on the right path
For my new skin shines
For my new skin is fresh
For my new skin is vibrant
Strong and better protected
Emerging from the inside out!

~ Suzie Nunes ~

As the Snow Fell Softly Around Me

As the snow fell softly around me, I started walking down the trail and up to the path that leads through the pines. There is a nice path going through the bush of pines. I stop to listen for a moment.

There are needles still on the pine trees, it is the middle of winter. So, as I am listening intently, I can hear the snowflakes falling (they are the big fluffy wet ones) down through the trees.

I never knew you could hear snow falling.

So, I stand there for a while just listening to that beautiful sound. It is so calming, so peaceful. I don't really want to carry on and keep walking, but I do anyway. I am just out here to go for a walk and listen to the sounds of nature.

As I carry on down the path, I can hear some birds chirping, but I can't see them. I look around to see if I can. I don't know all their songs so not sure who is doing the singing. So, I carry on walking down the trail.

Even though it is the middle of the afternoon, there is no one else on the trail. I think to myself that it is so beautiful out here and nobody else is here to enjoy it. If they only knew how peaceful it was out here.

~ Andrea Beaver Dennis ~

Today's Imagining

I am in this moment, simply choosing to be
Letting life unfold, revealed patiently
I have chased in the past, for answers and feelings
I understand now, life has a way of revealing,
Everything I need to know
To move forward and see my spirit flow.
Trusting that something greater is guiding
And when I stop looking, there can be finding.

Just for today is my only disposition,
Conscious contact keeps me in balanced position,
Moments passed, have lessons to drive me
I cannot go back, lamenting deprives me,
Of all the beauty in today,
Natural contrast of night and day
To be seen from the perspective I choose to see
A vision where simplicity aligns to agree.

The worry of tomorrow cannot exist
When I stop to simply feel, experience and persist
This moment is the only thing truly happening
I will create with the universe in today's imagining
I will allow the process and open my heart
Each moment I am in, a mindful start
A time to engage, discover, envision
Accepting my place in life's divine precision.

~ Lisa Colbert ~

On the Other Side of the Hill

On the other side of the hill I wonder what I will see. Should I take the step and find out? I think I should and do just that. So, I take the step and start climbing the hill. As I climb I start to look around.

What do I see? Well there are trees and green, green grass. There are also a few scattered farm houses. Some have fences, some have open fields and some have animals running around.

I keep walking up the hill, not really that much farther to go. I am getting excited, can't wait to get up there. It didn't really look that steep or long till I started the climb. As I keep walking it seems farther than it really is. I am about half way up. I keep walking. The air is so fresh and clean up here. I take in some deep breaths as I am walking. I love it, it feels so good.

Almost there. The view as I turn around to have another look at how far I have come is amazing. I can see a long way. I want to say for miles and miles but that of course is an exaggeration, laughing as I think that.

Just a few more steps and I am there. I stop, I close my eyes and I just breathe, for what seems like a very long time but is only minutes. I open my eyes and look around.

Can you just imagine the view?

It is a beautiful lake. Crystal clear water, you can almost see the bottom from up here. The waves are rolling into shore then back out again. There are people swimming and boating. I can hear them laughing and splashing and enjoying their day. I just stand here for a few minutes and take it all in and listen and enjoy. I decide to sit and just listen. It is calming, relaxing and brings a smile. Just what I need and what everyone should take the time to do.

~ Andrea Beaver Dennis ~

Windows to our soul

A deadly stare long and hard.
They reach into your heart,
Searching for some companionship.
So mysterious yet longing to be understood.

They understand and interpret so much,
Yet are still lost.
Lost in the world surrounding and hiding
The true compassion found within.

These mysterious tunnels are something we all own,
and are a reflection of what can be found within.
Of course, this true reflection of personality is found in one's eyes.

~ Jeff Martin ~

Nature Musings

As I stepped on the smooth path
I walked away from the house.
The stones on the path were worn smooth.
They were cold to the feet since I was barefoot.
The path wound around the trees.
Birds were in the trees chirping loudly.
The grass wasn't cut and was cool and spongy under my feet.
The path, once I got back on it, was leading toward the lake.
Six ducklings swam with their mother.
It was a peaceful scene with gentle, lapping water on the beach.
Farther down the beach were several swimmers out enjoying sunny rays.
One dog was frolicking on the beach with his owner, playing a game of fetch.

~ Valerie Malcovich ~

Changes

The clouds gusted slowly through the sky,
Blowing everything around it with reckless abandon.
Pizza boxes tossed into the air,
Random papers fluttering in their small tornadoes,
Through back alleys where only some dare to play,
Falling into the dark shadows of the stairwells and dumpsters.
Out on the street the newspaper stands rattle around,
While nearby the waves crash on the shore.

Nothing is safe from the clouds that deceivingly look so peaceful,
As they gust slowly through the sky,
Up above the world in slow motion they make their changes.

Where down here on the ground those changes almost seem accelerated,
Pushing through faster than sometimes is comfortable,
But sometimes that's what we need.

Comfortable is nice and change is scary.
But it's only when the pain of staying the same,
Becomes greater than the pain of change,
That we change.

Sometimes by then, that change is at such a painful place,
We are down on our knees, begging to be relieved of that burden.
When all it would have taken, was to recognize and surrender sooner.

But we struggle. By our nature we struggle for control.
Stubborn we think we can do it better.
And for those moments we delude ourselves and win.

Until life crashes down around us.
Forced to our roots we surrender,
And remember faith and love and hope.

Looking up at the clouds gusting in the sky,
I accept their changes,
Knowing it's inevitable and not on my terms anyway.

And for that I am grateful.
And with hope I turn over my will,
And ask for guidance.

~ Andrea Eygenraam ~

WINTER
Loss, Grief, Death & Faith

Memory Box

I open the box in front of me and discover a hard, smooth object wrapped in tissue paper, and I can tell by the touch that it is made of glass. Curious, I unwrap a delicate wine glass with a hexagonal shaped cup and a long stem. It has a small charm of a starfish around the base and I imagine it still holds a faint aroma of red wine.

My eyebrows furrow in confusion until suddenly a gasp escapes as I nearly drop the piece. In recognition, I close my eyes and a dim memory of my childhood bubbles to the surface. I am a little girl playing grown-up on New Year's Eve, pouring grape pop into the glass and drinking with my pinky up. I swirl the glass and giggle, sloshing the drink as I imitate the adults. I hold the glass to the side, pretending to study the colour of the liquid and suddenly the glass slips from my grasp and smashes on the floor. My beautiful grandmother rushes toward me, and guilty tears well up in my eyes, preparing for her anger, but she simply kisses my hands warmly and checks to see if I'm hurt. Her affection is surprising, and I cup her face gently as she kisses my palm, giggling again as she blows a raspberry against my fingers. The glass is broken, but I am whole again.

With a sigh I'm back to the box, my hands, still feeling the ghost of her kiss, idly unpacking and unwrapping items again, my mind wandering. I count four more wine glasses to a total of five, realizing she never replaced the one I broke. Like her, my future parties may need to be one guest fewer. And I find there's something strangely fitting about that. Digging deeper into the box, I uncover another item, this one wrapped in newspaper. I start to rip open the newspaper and realize it's a page from an old crossword puzzle. I check the date in the top corner, and I can feel the tears start welling up. I was never any good at those stupid things. Not like she was. Blinking quickly, I flatten the paper out on the table, attempting to smooth out the wrinkles. Perhaps I would put it in an old wooden frame and save this beautiful treasure, hang a small piece of her in my new apartment. She always loved the crosswords.

Unraveling the last of the newspaper, I uncover a green glass ash tray. The nostalgic smile I wear slowly fades to a frown. This, perhaps, is not such a lucky treasure to find. My thoughts spring to a dark day, one of the last ones before she left me. Her face had been gaunt then, not the vivacious one I had always known, so joyful and full of life. Her hair was falling out then, and I remember thinking it was strange that she should allow it to when she always took such pride in her locks, faithfully going to the hairdresser every Wednesday for her perm. But even though she deteriorated before me, she held onto her undeniable sense of humour, and demanded to know why the at-home caregivers who gave her sponge baths were never young hunky men. Then one day she looked up at me from her bed, and the words that she meant to say, the last goodbye, the last I love you, came out simply as "I like your jeans."

I snap back to the present with a start, still holding the ash tray, and hurl it across the room, smashing against the wall. Why would she give me this wretched thing?

A moment passes, and my ragged breathing gradually calms. The tears I am fighting to keep down cooperate and stay where they are, and slowly I regain control. Sighing, I get to my feet. I guess it's time to be a grown up again. I cross the room, and pick up shards of broken glass bare-handed, and scoop them into a pile. A piece slices into my cupped palm and I cry out, painfully dropping the fragments to the floor, tingling on the hardwood like singing, vengeful diamonds. Instinctively, I start raising my palm to my mouth, and pause. With a nostalgic smile, I kiss the wound lightly, blood smearing my lips, and blow a small raspberry into my palm. Though I'm alone, it makes me giggle. And it feels good.

I clean up the mess and put the empty box on a shelf, waiting to someday be filled with treasures of my own to pass down.

~ Jessica Schuler Feng ~

The White Box

I opened the box in front of me and discovered there was a mix-up. I did not recognize anything inside the small plain white box. A box that was no bigger than a shoebox but not quite as tall. A box that I thought was for me, that I was waiting for with anticipation. This mystery box now sat on my kitchen table. Inside was an incredible number of things, whoever packed this parcel packed it so strategically and well it was like Mary Poppins carpet bag, pulling out the impossible and yet there it lay; an explosion of memories on my kitchen table.

I stood there sweating a little trying to recall and think of how I am going to return each artifact into the box in such a way as to hide my impatient curiosity. It was like an exploded bomb; there were bits everywhere and I had no idea on how they all fit together. There is a large lace doily approximately 10" in diameter, it is that antique yellow all old things tend to turn. In contrast there sits a tiny blue IPOD, alone and with no headphones or charger and dead, quite upsetting actually, but that did not stop my exploration of the rest of the box's contents, did it?

There is an assortment of photographs filled with happy faces, hugs and a basset hound and one grey cat that keeps showing up in the corner or under a chair. Beautiful green eyes.

I see landmarks that tell me these were taken in Ontario. Things like the CN Tower, St. Jacob's Market sign and the Parliament buildings. There is are also random pieces of fabric. Most are an assortment of Teals and blues. The fabrics seem to be cotton with one exception. One piece that is silky smooth. It might even be silk.

Sitting in the middle of my table rests a tattered old envelope filled with stubs from various things like a ticket to Graceland, Giant's Causeway Tour, Maid of the Mist, a movie ticket from The Bucket List.

Odd, next to that there is a single cigarette that is so old it does not smell of tobacco but still sheds its content to the bottom of the box.

There is a single red 2$ Canadian bill, a looney, a toonie and 3 pennies with the year 1973 on them. There is a pen that has DALLAS along the side of it. It is a pen that clicks as the tip plays peek a boo depending if you click or double click...I like that sound. I should put it down.

Rolled up to the size of a face cloth is a white tank top with the head of Madonna on it, classic Madonna from the 80's, size small. There are some tattered postcards from Australia, Korea and Thailand and Spain. The ink on the other side has faded so much it is impossible to know who or what was attached to these snapshots in time.

All that could be made out is, Dear Jenny. All of it. All of these items rest on my table, all except two little items.

There all alone in the corner, almost hugging each other, are two pieces of jewelry staking their claim in the white box, this is their home, this is their safe place. The first is a simple gold Claddagh ring, the second a man's Casio watch, a nice one, the kind you would have to purchase in a jewelry store. On the back three words are etched: Love Loyalty Friendship.

Panic grips my throat as a microsecond of clarity whispers to me, "this is your box, these are your memories, hold on before you forget again Jenny" I look up and in the mirror and staring back are a pair of blue eyes, glistening with tears ready to fall.

These eyes fully aware of this moment, knowing in another microsecond it would all be gone...not the contents of the box but my memory.

A blink of my eyes and a breath. I open my eyes. I look down at my kitchen table and I open the box in front of me and discovered there was a mix-up. I did not recognize anything.

~ Jenny Kuspira ~

The Box

I opened the box in front of me and discovered
A bundle of memories wrapped in a ribbon
Stored away long ago to be preserved
I didn't know her to be overly sentimental
But here they are

The letters that were written
Some never to be seen by the named recipient
Some so raw that the words hurt even now
I let the ribbon fall away from the paper
My fingers tracing the familiar script
Her handwriting taught to her by her mother
And reinforced by teachers
Back when handwriting and cursive were still important teachings
Before technology took over
Back when letter writing was common practice
And the only way people found out the real stories
About what their family and friends were experiencing in far off lands
Or even just a short distance away
Because sometimes writing the words would be easier than saying them out loud

There is emotion in a letter
That you might never see in a Twitter tweet or Facebook post
Because you can write it freely
And then never mail it
But the words have been sent into the universe
Through the very nature of holding a pen and letting the words flow

I read through the pages in my hand, feeling her emotions
As the words are pulled from the past
Remembering those times she has written about

Feeling her pain
Remembering her joy
I read every one
She was so young when some of them are written

So naive
Some are written to her husband, her parents and her children
Some to herself

I read every one
Then I fold them neatly and bundle them up with the pretty ribbon
And place them back into the box
Carefully labelling it **MOM'S LETTERS**

Because someday when I am gone my children will want to know
Who she was
What she feared
What she felt
And what she aspired to become

It's all there
Written on lined paper in forgotten cursive script
Wrapped in a pretty ribbon
Waiting for them to discover
Their mother's younger self

~ Pamela Simmonds ~

Bag of Butterflies

"Bag of butterflies what nonsense," grumbled Gus on his way home. "Pardon me." A woman's voice interrupted. Gus continued "the idea that imagining butterflies will brighten your day, nonsense." "No. I would like to get off now." The woman speaking to Gus was a prisoner between all six foot four of him, and the window on the street car. She gave Gus a look that said "I really want to get off now."

Realizing he had continued his inner dialogue of disgust out loud with a stranger on a street car shocked Gus back into the reality of the moment. He shook his head once, apologized under his breath and moved across the aisle to over compensate the fact he was not trying to "start" anything. If anything, he was trying to shake off and forget the conversation he had with his friend. Instead though it looped over and over again, bag of butterflies, imagining happiness, ridiculous. Ding. It was finally his stop. Gus got off the street car and started to walk home. The looping continued and the butterfly debate swelled inside his mind all the way home. The rage and upset spread into his arms and his legs which propelled him home faster than he had been home in months. Gus swung the front door open with such force it could have been ripped off its hinges if the rust had not so been so deep and thorough.

"How could you?" cried a child's voice. It's shrillness cutting the fog in Gus's head. A moment later Gus realized it was little Diane. Little Diane his neighbor from across the hall. Little Diane who had known Gus all of her life, all 8 years of it. Little Diane in her overalls and braids. Little Diane who loved everyone and everything, especially insects and animals. Her voice was not shrill at all but in fact just a question from a child to her neighbor.

"You killed Joey"

"Pardon"

"You killed Joey. I don't think you meant to, but you did!" Gus's expression quickly changed from one of rage and anger to one of confusion, eyebrows raised and mouth open, but no words coming out. Without another word Diane took Gus by the hand and walked him back to the front entrance of their apartment building.

Diane stopped and looked at Gus, starting from his shiny black business shoes to his grey business suit and finally to the top of his head with his perfect hair which never moved or was out of place. Gus looked at Diane as Diane looked to the sidewalk. Gus followed Diane's gaze to a black spot on the sidewalk. It was not a large or symmetrical spot but it was definitely there, black against the grey pavement. Looking more closely Gus spotted many little legs and green ooze which he guessed were the insides of a bug…the insides of Joey. Joey was one of Diane's "friends". Gus now understood Diane's question and upset. Returning his gaze to Diane he uttered most sincerely, "I am sorry".

"It's not me you need to say sorry to," With a hop a skip and a jump Diane had returned to the mighty maple in front of their building. It was a beautiful tree whose branches reached up seemed to almost touch the sky, it was the perfect hotel for all of Diane's "friends". Diane held up a tray covered with mason jars filled with grass, leaves and black spots. These black spots were alive and moving about silently munching on the meal of green leaves and grass. Each jar had a strip of tape identifying each passenger proudly, below a lid of a saran wrap and elastics. Hilda, Pat, Kimmy, Rita and Carl – Joey had five family members apparently. An easy deduction as there was one Mason jar with grass and leaves, no lid or black spot but a piece of tape that read in large blue letters JOEY.

There was a pause; Diane and Gus locked eyes for a moment. "I am sorry." Gus repeated once more to Diane. He was not apologizing for killing Joey, but sorry for not having the strength to support Diane's naive joy in each living creature despite their multiple legs, tiny size and place in the world. Gus was sorry for being miserable, and sorry that he did not fully comprehend what just happened. Diane said nothing but instead continued the conversation Gus had obviously interrupted. "Don't you guys worry. Joey will still become a butterfly, just in heaven now…" Diane was back under the maple tree and Gus gratefully retreated to apartment 2B. Gus was glad this day had come to an end.

The trouble with a day ending a new one always begins. Gus just wanted to forget everything but the next morning things kind of went the opposite way. Gus's disgust and refusal to acknowledge anything to do with feelings, insects or Diane actually grew into a massive curiosity. It was a curiosity that was like a magnetic force that would attract him to his balcony. All of a sudden, coffee on the balcony was better, breakfast on the balcony was better, even just reading the paper was better on the balcony. Diane was often under the mighty maple tree or the front stoop with "the family". Gus became an unconscious and unwilling spy of the Family and Diane.
Gus didn't want to be a spy but every day Gus would watch Diane taking the time to get fresh grass and leaves, taking the time to care.
Diane was always either within his eye line or earshot. "Any day now" Gus could hear Diane speaking; they were just outside under his window enjoying the shade of the overhang of Gus's balcony. "I am so happy for you...you will be free and able to find Joey and fly together." With those words something clicked, something had shifted inside of Gus. He decided that he needed to speak with Diane, and it had to be soon.

It is important to understand that Gus liked order, things that made sense and are clean crisp and in place as well as keeping to himself. Gus disliked nonsense, fanciness, disorder, emotions, insects or anything dirty, but Gus did like Diane; he liked Diane quite a bit. He realized that he did hurt Diane and he really did feel bad about killing Joey. He now had a plan, an idea but was terrified to speak with this little girl.

"Today is the day, today is the day" Gus jumped out of bed, startled and drawn automatically straight for his balcony. It was 5:45am, and there sat Diane on the stoop with the Family on their tray. Diane was dressed in her usual blue jean overalls, a white t-shirt and two braids. She whispered to the family, "it is starting guys. do not worry. I am here. I will protect you. You are doing great."
Gus had not realized until now that all of the leaves were now replaced with a single twig in each jar with a single chrysalis hanging from it, except Joey's jar, which stood in its place, empty and clean.

Gus focused in on Kimmy's jar and saw that her chrysalis was twitching ever so slightly, then the bottom of it ripped open and out dropped Kimmy, Upside down at first, but then in the blink of an eye she corrected herself and sat on the outside of her twig, her body pulsating and pumping blood to the weak and damp wings on her back. Gus never saw anything so mesmerizing and beautiful. As if by magic the rest of the family did exactly the same as Kimmy until each were sitting upright and pulsating on their twigs, rhythmically. It was like a living Salvador Dali painting of butterfly dominos.

The time had arrived. The time for Gus to speak with Diane and put his plan into action...Looking at his watch again it was now 6:15. It was too early. Perhaps after breakfast, or lunch. After lunch it is. At 1200 noon Diane was still sitting on the stoop with the family. The wings now outstretched and delicate, starting to flap every so often. Gus somehow ended up sitting next to Diane on the stoop.
"Hey."
"Hey…look Gus" Diane was watching "Today is the day. They get to fly" As if on cue each of the family spread their wings, flapped them a few times, and found the top of the jar perching for a just a moment and then away they flew. Diane took photo after photo like a proud mama. Diane could neither look away nor stop smiling.
Gus once again followed her gaze but this time to the sky. "Are you sad?"
"Why would I be sad?" Averting his eyes to the ground where he first met Joey Gus uttered, "Joey. Are you sad that Joey is not here?"
"No. I'm ok"
Diane finally dropped her gaze from the sky to look at Gus. "I got to watch Pat, Kimmy, Rita, Carl and Hilda fly." Gus's silent confused look returned. Diane continued, "After all Joey was just a caterpillar but because of him I met his family and was able to watch them fly…how cool is that?"
"I see." Gus suddenly felt out of place and uncertain of what he planned. Had he read too much into what he saw and thought about Diane? Was it going to be a disaster, what he had planned? Gus's right hand started to fidget with a tiny blue velvet drawstring bag in his right jean pocket. Gus thought to himself, "I have come this far…I may as well finish this."

"I have something for you."

"Cool. What is it?"

"Before I give it to you I want to tell you a quick story. I have a friend; her name is Polly. One day not too long ago she told me about the Bag of Butterflies." Gus could not have said anything more intriguing for Diane, because she loved butterflies. "She told me that she always carries her bag of butterflies, especially for her friends who are sad and low. I asked to see it. Polly reached behind her back and pulled out nothing…just air. She then pretended to see butterflies. It upset me."

"Why"

"Because there was no bag, no butterflies just air. Polly then told me the butterflies are here and she started to jump around and smile, 'the bag of butterflies is magic' she said 'and can make anyone feel better, they just have to find their butterfly.'"

"I told her she was crazy. I then stormed off and came home." The pause in the story was so long that Diane, a very clever girl, concluded in her mind that was the day that Joey was killed.

"Here!" Gus presented Diane with the tiny blue velvet bag. "I thought you were sad so I thought maybe a bag with some magic butterflies would help"

Gently Diane opened the bag and looked inside. "There are no butterflies in here. There is just one butterfly. Wanna see??"

Gus looked inside and at first all he saw was the inside of the velvet bag…then somehow, he saw it he really did, there was one butterfly; One beautiful butterfly.

"Thank you, Gus, thank you for bringing me Joey; I will keep him with me always." No more words, just a look and a wave and Diane returned to the maple tree in the yard. Standing silently Gus watched as Diane gently placed the velvet bag in her pocket. Gus realized that he was smiling ear to ear not because of Diane, but because of Joey. Joey helped Gus to learn and understand that not all butterflies can be seen but all butterflies can be felt, in the belly, in the heart and in the mind and they are all spectacular. Gus quietly lifted his bag of butterflies and slung it over his shoulder and headed back to apartment 2B.

~ Jenny Kuspira ~

Gone

Hold a life in the palm of your hand
Watch it drip away, cover the land
Around you a lake of your sins, hopes, and fears
Until that lake hits your nose, your ears
You begin to drown in a bittersweet abyss
It's death's unjustified and fatalistic kiss.
It cradles you softly, a babe wrapped in warmth
Until it surrounds you, chokes out your life force
Your heart that was just beating a rapid pace
Begins to slow, to fade, just empty space
Your eyes flutter shut as you fall asleep
You'll never wake again, to smile, to weep
It's the end of your story, your life-long tale
And you leave behind loved-ones to weep and whail
But you sit in the sky and watch them all grow
From blooms, to sun, to golden leaves, to snow
As their lives move on with great success
You smile to yourself, and finally let yourself rest.

~ Jodi Cronyn ~

The Last Summer

This was where it had happened so it was only fitting that she should rest here forever. It was her favourite spot, after all. Their faithful friend watched from the dock as he maneuvered the small craft to the precise spot where the boy on the Sea-Doo had clipped her while she was swimming back from a day on the island. She was a strong swimmer; traversing the channel many times in her twenty plus years of coming here. She loved swimming. Almost as much as she loved the waterfront cottage and the old hound waiting on the dock. It had never crossed his mind that his daughter might die here. The finality of it still weighing heavy on his heart. A man should never have to lay his child to rest. Parents aren't supposed to outlive their children. He was the only one left now. Cancer had stolen his wife just last year. Just him and Jack now. All promise of grandchildren washing away with the ashes riding the waves. Sadness engulfed him as he emptied the last of her remains in the waning sunset. He sat there for a moment lost in contemplation. Letting out a little yelp from the dock, Jack jerked him back to the present. The paddles silently cut through the water while ashes swirled on the surface. Teary eyed his eyes met Jack's, "Well Boy, I guess that's that." As the last of the remaining light disappeared behind the island they coasted the length of the driveway, turning left at the Shady Shores street sign and settled in for the long drive back to civilization.

~ Pamela Simmonds ~

Oi
A story of coming alive

It was completely and utterly hopeless. Never in my life had I felt more like a failure than in that moment. Some adult I turned out to be – I couldn't even make it through two months on my own without help from mommy and daddy. Pathetic, was what it was. I had literally zero dollars, or in this case euros, to my name; no food, no place to stay, and there was an ocean between home and me.

At eighteen years old, I bought a one-way ticket to Europe and never wanted to look back. My parents, obviously upset with my decision to leave and forgo university and any concrete plans for my future, cut me off. "Go try to make it on your own, see how far you get," my father had said. So I left, two weeks after my birthday, with only what I could carry on my back and the little nest egg of money I saved up from my part time job. I had no plan other than to run, to get away from this boring and repressive place and find adventure. I can't recall ever being so terrified. It was the first time I had ever travelled on my own, and the first time I had been overseas. My understanding of currency exchange, foreign language and customs was limited, to say the least. Yet, there I sat, with a window seat, on a jet headed to London.

Which brought me to this moment, sitting on a step outside of Katz Castle on the Rhine River, tears streaming down my face. It happened just like he said it would - I couldn't make it on my own.

"Oi! Darlin', you best be careful, the whole world's gonna see your soul through those tears". The 'oi' didn't match the Mississippi accent, but it did match the crooked grin and playful, but concerned, eyes. Normally, I would be embarrassed at being caught crying, especially by a stranger, but all I could do is look up at him. Words were caught in my throat, sitting behind that lump that screamed, "My father was right".

I figured when I didn't reply, he would just go away – I'd seen my fair share of broken souls and kept on my way – but to my surprise, he sat down beside me and pulled out a cigarette. "Do you mind?" he asked, before lighting up. I shook my head and looked down at my hands.

This may have been, by far, the most awkward and most comfortable situation I had been in since arriving in Europe, sitting here, crying, next to some stranger blowing smoke rings into the air. We sat there in silence, for what seemed like hours, but I'm sure was only minutes. I know what some of you may be thinking – a young girl, alone in a foreign country, obviously vulnerable, sitting next to a stranger, perhaps wasn't the safest situation. In that moment, though, I knew I was safe. It wasn't something I could logically explain, but my heart and my gut felt safe.

"The doctors told me twenty-two months ago that I have an inoperable brain tumor," he stated, breaking the silence, "and I'm not gonna live to see thirty. I always wanted to see the world, so I've been travelling ever since."

It was such an unexpected statement that I didn't know how to respond, all I could do was just look at him. In his eyes there was no agenda, no need for anything, just an openness that I had never really experienced before.

"I'm gonna head into the village for a bite, you wanna join me?" he asked.

This brought a new onslaught of tears, and I blurted out, "I have no money to buy food." Immediately, I was ashamed and brought my hands to my face, trying unsuccessfully to hide my tears.

He didn't in any way touch me, and I couldn't see his face through my hands, but I heard him say, "Well, at least now I know you speak English. Why don't I buy you some lunch and we can talk?"

"I don't want to talk about it," I immediately retorted, likely with more defensiveness than was necessary.

"Maybe I need someone to talk to," he said quietly.

I did look up at him then, wiping my tears away, trying to read his expression. His eyes were brown, that kind of brown that looks like chocolate one moment, and golden the next. They looked out from under scraggly hair that was also brown with a hint of gold. That crooked smile was back, showing equally crooked teeth with a gap in the front, making an otherwise standardly handsome face seem more real. His shirt was red with a surfboard on it, and along his forearm was a tattoo that read "all you have is this moment". Little did I know, this was one of the most pivotal moments of my life thus far.

I took a deep breath, knowing my options were limited, and said, "Okay."

We walked through the countryside into town, him telling me tales of his travels through Australia, New Zealand, South East Asia, and Eastern Europe. Two hours of conversation later, we were sitting in Café Loreley, eating spritzkuchen, my tears long dried, and my worries pushed to the back of my mind. This man, Lex was his name – short for Alexander, which is said was too stuffy – had led this unbelievable and inspiring life. He had learned to surf in Australia, dove the Great Barrier Reef, climbed Mount Tasman, helped build homes in several Asian countries, and danced the night away at some of the best festivals in the world. As he sat there, telling me about his life, you would never know this was a man who was told he would die at any time within the next three years. He was relaxed, open, alive, and just excited about everything. If I had been given that news, I would likely be holed up in a corner absolutely terrified. In so many ways, he epitomized life.

Soon, I found myself smiling and laughing and beginning to relax into his infectious energy. I had never met anyone like him before, and I was in awe of the adventures and images his stories were creating in my mind and heart.

"So, you don't end up sitting on the stairs of Katz Castle in tears without there being a story," he prompted, sitting across from me with his chin resting on his folded hands. For a moment, it all came rushing back – the hopelessness, the fear – but he reached over and gently placed his hand on mine. No expectations were in that touch, just comfort and assurance. I had never met a man who didn't have any expectations of me before, and I felt something new in my heart; a strange little spark that I couldn't really explain.

So, my story came out. Just as he told me of his adventures, I told him of my own – the trains of England, the rolling hills and cliffs of Scotland, the four days in Amsterdam I couldn't recall (I apparently had a very good time), and my arrival and exploration of Dusseldorf. When I came to the story of how I ended up at Katz Castle with no money, stranded with no one to help me, I couldn't speak. The words were stuck in my throat again and the tears began to well once more. It was easy to forget, in this warm and inviting little café, sitting across from this friendly and eager stranger, everything that had happened. It was easy to forget that I still had no idea what to do.

Reaching into his pocket, he pulled out a hanky – yes, an honest-to-god hanky – and handed it to me, again placing his hand on mine. "Listen, you don't have to tell me this part of your story." The crooked smile had left and was replaced with a look of concern and contemplation. "It seems like you're in a really tough spot, and I know what that's like. Sometimes we need a little help in life, and that's ok. You don't always have to do everything on your own."

"I can't ask you for help," I said quietly, not able to look him in the eye.

He smiled again and replied, "You didn't ask, I'm offering. Look, I'm staying here for a couple nights, I have my room booked, and then I'm heading down river to work on a vineyard for a week. I'm sure they have room for another worker, you can make a bit of money, and then figure out your next move."

There was a part of me, the part that all of us women have, that was hesitant. All my life, I had been taught to be wary of men, that they only want one thing, and I was very vulnerable and desperate at the moment. I didn't necessarily trust my own judgment. Yet, he sat there looking so sincere, and my heart didn't feel afraid of him.

"Okay," I finally breathed, watching his face fall back into that crooked smile.

He paid the bill, and we made our way back through the countryside, to the next village where he was staying. Not knowing really what to say, I was quiet as he told me in detail about his future travel plans – bungee jumping off a bridge, skiing the Swiss Alps, tasting the food in France, laying under the stars in Tuscany, island hopping in Greece, and diving with sharks in the Mediterranean, were just a few of the items on his list. He didn't want to miss anything. To me, this all sounded so beautiful, and absolutely terrifying. Though I wanted adventure, I realized I had still been playing it safe, not able to fully let myself go and absorb in these new experiences.

The room he was staying in was simple, but he had left his mark. There were clothes lying on the floor by the bed, a harmonica sitting on the table with a half-drunk bottle of wine, a journal with messy writing sitting open beside it. He made no apologies about the mess, and I needed none. This room, though only a temporary home, told me much about him, and I liked all of it. I felt awkward, though, standing in the middle of his room, my backpack in one hand and my guitar in the other, not knowing quite what to do. This wasn't my space, and I had just met this person.

Reaching out, he took my guitar and set it on the chair, and said, "Make yourself at home, I'm gonna pop downstairs and get some things for dinner. If you wanna freshen up or do whatever it is you women folk do, go ahead."

That made me smile, and as soon as he left, I went into the bathroom, locking the door behind me. It had been three days since I had a proper shower, and I did take a bit of time just enjoying the warm water. When I finally looked in the mirror, I was a bit startled at how tired I looked. For a girl of eighteen, I certainly was showing a little wear and tear. Vanity prevailed, and I braided my hair and put on a bit of makeup. I couldn't figure out why, I didn't want to give this guy the wrong impression, but I suppose the beauty programming runs deep.

Lex had returned when I came out, and was cutting up some cheese, bread, and sausages, music playing from the stereo – Stone Temple Pilots. Humming along to the music, he moved around almost as if I wasn't there, and I couldn't tell if he was giving me space to adjust, or if he was just that person who was always comfortable and didn't need to fill the silence. Maybe both. "Would you like to open the wine and pour a glass?" he asked. That earned him big points in my mind. He knew enough not to have already opened the wine and offer me a glass, showing me, again, that he really intended no harm.

As we sat over food and wine at the tiny table that evening, I began to let my guard down, opening up about my past. The conversation turned to music when he mentioned my guitar, and we found we liked many of the same musicians. "Would you play something for me?" he asked.

Again, I found myself feeling a bit of shame – my own musical abilities brought up a lot of insecurity. Playing for someone was like laying out my heart for others to critique, and my heart wasn't necessarily in a place for that, especially in that moment. Intuitively, he seemed to realize he was asking a lot, so he said, "Why don't I play a bit on my harmonica, and you join in? We can have some fun with it and see what we come up with!" That infectious and excited energy he had was back, and I agreed with a laugh.

We spent three hours that night making music, laughing, and joking that we could start a band called the Wandering Ramblers. For the first time in a very long time, almost my whole life, I felt like I could be the real me. The weird, artistic, perceptive, and intuitive woman, who craved adventure, was allowed space to exist.

A yawn overcame me, and I immediately felt awkward again as he mentioned sleep. There was only one bed. That insecurity was eased when he grabbed one of the pillows and curled up on the tiny futon, leaving the bed for me. As a laid there, sleep eluding me, I couldn't help but continuously ask myself what I was doing and whether this guy was actually for real. I was lying in a room with a man I had only known for fourteen hours. Surely, I was crazy, and falling asleep was not the best idea, but eventually that heaviness that comes with deep exhaustion claimed me.

I awoke to the smell of coffee and fresh bread, and sat up, looking around the room. The bathroom door was closed and I could hear the shower. Sun was shining through the window, and I saw the source of that delicious fresh bread smell sitting on the table with a small selection of homemade jams. My belly rumbled. Again, that feeling of awkwardness at being in this strange man's room fell on my shoulders, and I didn't know whether to help myself or wait. If we had slept together, I would've helped myself with no second thought, but this man didn't seem to want anything from me, and I wasn't used to that.

Thankfully, he popped out of the bathroom, saying, "Help yourself to breakfast. The coffee is a bit questionable, but the bread and jams are delicious." He plopped down at the table with his own coffee and began buttering a piece of bread, making me smile at his utter ease and contentment.

"Just let me freshen up and I'll join you," I replied, grabbing my bag and heading into the bathroom. Again, I looked in the mirror, looking myself in the eye, and made the choice to trust this man. I had no one else, and he had done nothing to show me I couldn't put a little faith in him.

When I came out into the main room, he was on the balcony with his journal and cigarette, so I took that time to come back to a morning ritual I had let go of for the past few days. I grabbed coffee and a couple of pieces of bread, and then sat down at the table with my guitar. Music was my therapy, and after the past few days, it was needed.

He sat at the table with his journal when he came back in, not saying a word, allowing me space. It was the first moment I wondered if he felt as awkward as I did with this entire arrangement. I closed my eyes, strumming my guitar, and allowed myself to just be with my thoughts. This man, he knew he was going to die, and so he wasn't afraid to live. Everything he did, every word, every movement, even his stillness and silence, was filled with life, and he made me want to be alive. He was the first person who made me believe that life was a beautiful adventure, and that all things were possible.

Suddenly, he looked up at me over his coffee as I was lost in the moment with my guitar, and asked, 'What do you want to do today?'

I stopped, taking in his face, his complete ease and openness, and smiled, making the most important decision of my life.

"Everything. I want to do everything."

That was the moment I made the choice to really live

~ Jodi Cronyn ~

Leaves

The door creaked open and one leaf fell in front of me on my path and...
I am reminded of these wise words: "Life comes from death, nothing is alive that wasn't dead."
Hard words to hear when you are heart broken,
but he only spoke the truth.
He was a wise man, could see beyond the veil,
knew for a fact there is life after death,
and lived accordingly.

I sat, stunned, in his studio, wondering why, why, why?
Why do we have to deal with death?
Why do we need to learn to live without loved ones?
Why could I not be granted more time with my father?
Why, after learning how to be great friends did I lose him?

Some answers have become clear
and I have learned to live without him, in the flesh.
My father is in my life every single minute of it
and my love for him has only strengthened.

Falling leaves remind me of life cycles
and I am learning to live following the principle
that while death is everywhere, so is rebirth
Life is an amazing force
and I am writing this while sitting in my garden,
in awe of the adaptability that the plants are showing
at this particular time: ready to die,
to follow their natural cycle but given extra warmth and light,
ready to burst with life over and over again.

Death did not defeat me, although at one point it almost did.

I burst out to life again, and I am grateful I did.

~ Elena Pastura ~

Mother's Day 2010

This year marks the 10th Mother's Day without you.
I really don't know what to think, say or even do.
I remember 10 years ago when your magnolia just wouldn't bloom,
It missed you too
I think it's safe to assume.
There have been so many mixed feelings over the years,
Anger, laughter, confusion and a lot of tears,
Tears of sadness, joy and bittersweet freedom.
Acceptance for everything has started to come.
Although the path to get here has been long and hard,
And it hasn't been easy letting down my guard,
It's been so worth it, to be this new person.
With these old toxic ways you taught me, I'm more than done.
I kiss those painful memories goodbye,
And finally let go a deep and healing sigh

~ Andrea Eygenraam ~

FIRE

Burning Away the Pain to Rise like the Phoenix

Wild

I look out from the dock, watching him intensely, concerned for his safety. The man I love is rowing a canoe in the middle of a sparkling lake, sitting in the boat and watching the sun purple the clouds as it sinks back toward the horizon. A low whine escapes my throat, beckoning him to return to me, and I pace anxiously back and forth across the wooden boards, my eyes still glued to his face.

"Be a good girl now," He calls out to me from the boat. "I'm just going for a quick row to the other side. I'll be back in no time." With a few powerful strokes of oars, he speeds off toward the sunset, and I watch him disappear into a tiny speck on the horizon, never moving from my place. I sit on my haunches, attempting to wait patiently and control my constant trembling, but the unrelenting urge to move prevents me from relaxing entirely. I get up to my feet again and squint toward the sunset, unable to enjoy any of its beauty, trying to detect any sign of his return with my keen eyes, but to no avail. Surely, he must be on his way back by now. Why could I not go with him?

Frustrated, I begin pacing back and forth across the boards again, my feet padding softly on the weathered wood, when a long, chilling howl ripples out from the forest behind me. My muscles freeze in place, but I lift my nose to the air and taste their scent on the wind.

There are many of them, others, but not exactly like me. There is wildness in their song that I haven't felt in a long time, and I can sense certain feeling of yearning from them. Of desperation. They are not far from me.

Panic courses through my body, spurring me into action, and I sprint from the dock back toward the dense forest. I pray that my love will be safe in his boat, but I cannot win a fight against these Others who would surely find me standing in the open like this. Frantically I run, searching for a place to hide, for a place they will not detect me, but grow more desperate by the minute. I find a little space among the roots at the base of an enormous oak tree, and wriggle inside, wedging my body as far into the heart of the tree as I can manage, smearing mud on my shiny white coat in the process. I turn around and around in my crawl space and try to curl my body into a ball, relaxing as best I can in the cramped place. Somehow, I instinctively know that these Others are bigger than me and will not reach me here, and my frayed nerves ease a little, though I am still sick with worry over my love, alone in the canoe. I have no other choice but do my best to relax.

What feels like several hours pass, and I do not hear that chilling song again. Once in the night I suspected that they stood curiously outside my hiding place, drawn by my scent, but if they did, they never attempted to pry me from my safety and must have moved on. My body is frozen in place, and I am terrified to move for a long time, until eventually I manage a quick peek outside through the roots and dirt. The forest seems deserted, so I gather my courage and start the process of wriggling free of the hidey hole. Once out, I stretch expansively, my body tight and sore from the confined place, but my heart is glad to have survived the night relatively unscathed. I can see my love again! Racing as fast as my cramped legs can carry me, I find my way through the forest back toward the dock, retracing my steps as quickly as I can. The sun is just beginning to peek out over the horizon, slowly waking up from its peaceful sleep. My heart pounds with excitement and my panting increases as I finally reach the dock, scanning the water frantically. Where is he? Where is he?!

Suddenly the metallic scent of blood strikes me like a thunderclap, and I rush toward it, terror and dread filling my heart. Near the dock, my love's untethered canoe floats, washed to the shore by gently rippling waves. There, in the middle of the boat, was his blood, a vast pool of it, darkening the interior. I shove my muzzle into it and sniff, staining my light fur a deep crimson, and I howl. My broken heart explodes through my throat, my voice a song of agony, soaring higher and higher into an aching crescendo, beautiful and terrible in its pain, and I care no longer for this world. I howl out again and again until my voice is ragged and spent, and I collapse exhausted in the canoe, my soul weeping.

A gentle touch on my side startles me from my pain, and I look up. One of the Others stands beside me. He regards me with slanted, curious eyes that beckon me, that promise me a new life, a life of running and singing and dancing in the forest. A life of the wilderness. Some ancient yearning stirs in my chest, some unheeded call I held within me my entire life that I didn't realize was there. I get to my feet and follow him into the forest. Perhaps there may be more for me after all.

~ Jessica Schuler-Feng ~

The Wolf Pack

I felt the hair on my arms stand up
when I saw those dark eyes staring at me.
The grey fur also standing up.
As I slowly drew near it I could see in its eyes,
the wolf staring back at me.
Like he knew I wasn't there to harm him.
Like he was a part of me.
The moon was shining brightly down upon us.
And then so gently he began to howl.
And I ended up chiming in.
He was calling to his pack.
To the family he cares for.
The friends he loved.
It still makes my hair crawl.
It was like he was a part of me.
The lone wolf searching for his pack.
 I know one day I will find mine.
I must.

~ Keith Withers ~

As the Leaves Blew

It was a blustery autumn day where the weather was constantly changing and you were never sure how to dress.
I was walking down the street as the leaves rained down on me from all the trees overhead, shedding their coats for the fall. Their colours muted at this time of year, yet still providing a stunning back drop to the fall scene I was walking through.
As I breathed in the crisp fall air and surveyed my surroundings, I spotted the most striking woman walking toward me. She had on a pure white fur coat, not touched by the weather, as if she had a forcefield protecting her. She had on kitten heels, helping her walk with authority, that was clearly self-proclaimed, although very convincing and captivating.
The leaves seemed to also respect this space around her and not a leaf touched her pure white cloak. As she strutted, she had a nasty little smile, commanding the street. The leaves moved out of her way as did everything else, except me.
I was standing frozen, stunned, mesmerized, curious.
Who was she and where did she come from?
It was autumn, when the veil is the thinnest and strange things happen with spirit
For a moment I was reminded of Raul Dahl's The Witches, but I had a sense she meant no harm, despite that mischievous smile.
I wanted to know more, but didn't dare approach her. I couldn't speak – my voice squeaked when I tried
She laughed a whole-hearted belly laugh and said "Darling, come here, you have much to learn."

~ Andrea Eygenraam ~

Bitch You Don't Know Me

Bitch, you don't know me!
You think you have it all figured out
But you really have no clue.
See, you think it's all about you.

Don't you dare look at me
With those judgmental eyes.
Or litter the world
With your fucking lies.
'Cause Bitch, you don't know me!

Bitch, you don't know me!
You don't know my past.
You don't know
What I've been through.
Or why I will last.

You see, my life has been challenging
And I've learned to survive.
But you can't even see
Past your own little life.

Try walking a mile
In my shoes.
Just take a little walk
Through my memories
And see what you would do.
,Cause Bitch, you don't know me!
Do you?

~ Pamela Simmonds ~

Silent Serpent

The serpent is circling, silent and slow,
Patient and cunning, staying hidden down low,
Encircling wide, with a smile full of charm,
Gently and softly, curling round one arm.
Mesmerizing; as the gaze is met,
Not revealing any sense of danger yet,
As the grip tightens ever so slight,
It sends a shiver that doesn't seem quite right,
Softly the snake slithers, massaging down the spine,
The tail at the neck brings discomfort - but it's fine.
Around the chest the circle is made,
The pressure is squeezing making breath fade,
How did the creature become so bold?
The warmth is gone consumed by cold.
Soon little is left, spirit is fading,
The soul that was strong and energy creating,
Pulls from the last ounce of strength and self-worth,
Breaks free from the snake, as it falls to the earth.
A hawk swiftly dives in high from above,
Soaring off with the serpent, and looking back with love.

~ Lisa Colbert ~

By the Big Old Bulldog

Blood on my lips.
Buried it.
A little under.
By the yellow bloom.
Hoped it would grow.
Gone too soon.
By the big old bulldog,
The softer memories.
Lit a candle.
Lit a candle.

I couldn't have waited any longer,
if I was stronger, maybe so much time,
for not enough time, to be stronger.
Gone too soon,
by the big old bulldog,
the softer memories.
Lit a candle watched the flame.

I'm only one person,
looking on and cursin' these circles that grow too small,
and never happened, couldn't happen.
Car starts out back at the coffee shop,
rear of the garden, another brake squeaking,
waiting for the cat to come home.

Don't want to be alone with this
might have been mosquito memory.
Gone too soon.
Buried it by the big old bulldog,
softer memories.
Lit a candle.

~ Sarah Farr ~

Lyra

I know you are in rainbows and the glitter in the snow,
How is it I miss someone I never got to know?
I can see you tiny fingers and recall touching your toes,
Wishing you would take a breath, you were just not meant to grow,
At least not as my little one, perfect in tiny form,
I want to embrace those memories finding somewhere warm,
But my tears fall cold; and winter is too near;
Resisting the sadness quickly blocked by fear,
This does not honour you nor connect me to true self,
You are so much more than the memory box sitting on a shelf,
You remind of my strength and that I can face nightmares on my own,
Now to reach out through my pain and accept I'm not alone.
Sorrow is a process that is not within control,
Resistance and isolation is what will take its toll,
Allowing for the heartbreak to come then wash away,
Will help me to see your presence in my every day,
I will recognize your spirit lives in all of nature's gifts
I will allow the pain that's mine with faith that spirit lifts,
You exist always in the love you brought my heart,
That can never be lost, it existed deeply from the start.

~ Lisa Colbert ~

Doorway

I stood in front of the open door to the pastel painted nursery. The room was a soft green with white trim around the windows and baseboards.
I stood in the door and hesitated to enter, looking inside. There was a crib under a window that looked out to a yard with trees. Soft rain pattered against the pane, a light breeze whispering amongst the leaves and branches outside.
I'm not sure I have the courage to go inside. To look inside the bassinette. But I can't distract myself by looking around the room any longer, and my feet move ahead without my permission. My brain is uncertain, my heart is wounded, but my feet know where to take me, to the edge of the crib.
I take a deep breath, and see only a pile of soft blankets. Nothing stirs.
As tears sting the corners of my eyes, and I turn to walk out the room and lock the door forever, a little gurgle echoes from the crib. I turn, in amazement.
There lays my daughter, smelling of power, smiling up at me, looking at me with luminous eyes. Eyes that say I trust you to take care of me. Eyes that promise a future of tears as well as laughter. Eyes that believe in me to make her future bright.
I blink my eyes, tears welling up in the corners, and suddenly she is gone. And I am left wondering, was she ever really there at all?

~ Jessica Schuler-Feng ~

The Holes

People who think they feel nothing
When I have felt nothing I've actually felt too many things at once and shut down
The feelings overwhelm to a point of making me numb
I can't decipher one from the next
And I give up
Feeling imprisoned by my own thoughts
Handcuffed to memories trip wiring anxieties
Leaving me breathless, confused and lost
"Help!" I shout, silently from in my head
No one hears a sound
I can scream as loud as I want but the pain does not let a sound escape
Wanting to cry but no tears escape
They burn into my soul, causing holes
Wounds, traumas, deep inside
Wanting to heal but I can't fill them with silly putty
They must be filled with love
But in the darkness of my prison I cannot find the light to let the love in
The holes burn deeper
The darkness fills them with emptiness
Lost in memories down never ending hallways
Doors leading to escape are all lost
I shout down the hall and the echo dies in my heart
The sonic reverberation of my cries vibrate my heart back to life
There's a glimmer of love, of light
Light floods out from underneath a door closed down the hall
I run towards it as fast as I can
Like a superhero avoiding the laser traps
Rolling under alarm trip wires stealthy and speedy toward my goal
The light, I see it, it will be mine
Running from the prison of my mind toward freedom
Reaching the door, turning the knob, and bursting the door open
Only to find a mirror and realizing
I was never in a prison
The answers, the light, the love, were all in me all along
The feelings are all my own and I can choose what I will let in
I am filled with gratitude and love
And I sit contentedly in the open door that awaits

~ Andrea Eygenraam ~

AIR

Lifting up and Empowering

The Necessity of the Sunrise

They say the sun is a star?!
Is that right?
How can the sun be a star and the sun?
How can it be everything?
It's hot.
It's bright.
Its heat can be felt as far as this 3rd rock in the solar system called Earth.

I will believe what they say.
I will tell you what I know.
The sun has two beautiful gowns; one is called sunset and one is called sunrise.
Both are breathtaking and mesmerizing.

One is slightly more important.
The necessity of the sunrise gown is to open your eyes, to show you what lays ahead, your joy and your adventure.

The sunset gown cloaks the end of the day to provide you with a moment of gratitude, reflection and appreciation of the day that has just past.

Both are bright bookends to our days.
The necessity of the sunrise is so we can live.

~ Jenny Kuspira ~

Daybreak

Sometimes the universe allows you to see her
unbelievably beautiful colours
a haze of pink, orange, and purple
stop and just simply look up
stop and listen in silence
hear what she is telling you
how insignificant you really are

Free Moon

I long to see your beauty shine down on me

you are mesmerizing
take my
hopes and dreams
make me believe they can be reality
night after night
I can't resist a smile as I gaze in your direction

as you warm my heart

~ Diane O. Taylor ~

Paradise

When I step forward and prepare to take the leap, I nervously allow myself a tiny glance downward at my surroundings. My breath catches and eyes open wide when I realize I am standing at the top of a glorious cliff, poised atop a vast precipice.

Paradise lies before me. Lush forests spread across the land, rippling in green waves across vast rolling hills. A babbling river speeds through rocky terrain, never ceasing its steady course, insistently rushing, splashing, sloshing its way toward the distant ocean on the horizon who beckons to the river with its welcoming smile.

A light breeze stirs, lifting my hair and entwining it. For a moment, I lift an arm to pat it down, self-conscious of the tangle, but let my hand fall, and raise my chin to the clear sky, staring at the sun. She is a round orb, staring back. Unlike me, her gaze does not waver. She is strong, sure of herself. Her stare stings my eyes and I look away, painful and ashamed. Why did I come here? Who is it I am meant to be?

I rock unsteadily on my feet, weary of holding my body upright. Weary of being strong and being uncertain. Weary of many things. With a small sigh, I let my body fall, unable to stand any longer. Tears flow from my eyes as I speed downwards, but I fight to keep them open, watching as I plummet toward the paradise below me. My body is in free fall, and it feels good to completely let go, to have no further cares, no further weight pulling me down. The ground rushes up to me, and I prepare my body for the impact. To die in such a place would not be such a waste. To die seeing where the ocean meets the sky isn't so bad... right?

Suddenly, a stronger gust of wind whips through my hair again, and this time, I love the wild way it feels. I raise my chin to the sky once more, and I feel like I can fight again. Like I can be myself again. My eyes reflect the clear blue of the sky above me, and suddenly, I am a goddess. Spreading my wings, I open my heart to the world once more, and I soar.

The sun, smiling her knowing smile, tucks behind a cloud.

~ Jessica Schuler-Feng ~

A Seagull's Flight

The rising sun
With potential, even though it is unseen.
Slowly peeking through.

Whispering above the edge.
A new day is about to dawn.
A soft glimmer begins to shine through.

The crashing waves do not disturb.
Tranquility poised on the horizons crest
A seagull flies but unable still.

The altitude developing,
We are able to see,
The whispers dee revealing possibility.

A brilliant presentation
Of potential we first couldn't see.
Now in full bloom, the commotion is hiding so deep.

Colors blending,
An orchestra it looks to me.
The potential achieved and surpassed.

The seagulls continue to argue and bicker,
Till the late ends they do depart.
The radiance dimmed to dusk.

Looking out, off the windowsill,
You can pray knowing that,
Even though you can not see,
Tomorrow's crest holds a whisper of possibility.

~ Jeff Martin ~

Between Heaven and Earth

Between heaven and earth
Between heaven and earth
the stars above
the oceans below
the clouds above
the sea creatures below
the wind blows
the leaves rustle
the waves roll into the shore
look up at the sky
look down the shore
see the seashells
hear the wind
hear the waves gently rolling
in and back out
sit on the shore and
take it all in
what a wonderful way to
spend some time

~ Andrea Beaver Dennis ~

A Little Speck

A little speck encircled by all.
So tiny no one seems to notice at all.
Seeming to be lost in the chaos of Life's sea.

But there is love all around the speck to see,
Something hard for the speck to do.
Perhaps unconscious of it but still surrounded to see

This confusion in life distracting the speck so,
I all honesty it doesn't know where to go!
It's lonely and tired, life seems to go amiss.

Life for this little speck is uncertainty, definitely to be.
How does what appear to be a little speck live it fully through?
Does this little speck make a difference to you?

Again, reminded about the uncertainty, what to do?
Hard to feel certainty without feeling a little Mr. Magoo.
Questions. Questions. Questions.

It has no answers which are easily found.
Just questions begging for it to see.
How does a little speck live life as it was meant to be?

The speck goes here, the speck goes there.
It seems to have gone everywhere.
All around it tries to be but is still unable to see.

I often feel like a little speck, and am sure you do too.
Discovering the importance of you and of me
is something we have to see.
Get this to be something that comes naturally.

Many specks in this world make it a better place to be.
If you can only make a difference in a little specks life today,
You will finally be able to see.
A speck in the world is not all you are meant to be!

~ Jeff Martin ~

WATER

The Life Essence of Who We All Are

Do you know what you want?

Could it be? Is it really true?
That when you want something you just go get it or make it happen?

Quite often we dream about things we want and then somehow talk ourselves out of it for one reason or another, money being one of those reasons.

Money really is not a factor. I mean, yes, you do need some money to get by in this world but it is definitely not the determining factor.

The challenge is mostly in the figuring out what it is you truly want and getting clear on it.

Once you have a picture of this in your mind, or make a vision board, a dream board of sorts the toughest part is done.

Now gradually your wants begin to come to light.

It's easy to fall back into past patterns or self-sabotage so it's imperative that you identify when it's happening and steer yourself back on track.

At first the process seems slow, simply because it's a new way of doing things, practice, practice, practice and of course patience.

You most likely will experience trials and tribulations along the way but it is all part of the process.

Those trials are put there to teach you lessons, they are meant to help you.

Sometimes you feel like, "man I've been through this before why is it happening again?"

It's because you need to go through it again to peel back the layers of old wounds and experience these similar trials but this time with a new perspective and much more confidence and clarity.

Then one day it occurs to you that some of things you had been visualizing for your future life are in fact manifesting and showing up in your life.

Your aspirations and your goals are being realized!

What's more is by this time you will have gotten really good at manifesting what your heart truly desires.

It is fabulously rewarding.

I understand now that it is continual, life is like an ocean expanding and receding, rough or calm, but we are never done dreaming, we never get it all perfectly together, and when you think about it, that's the true beauty of it.

These days my ocean is fairly calm and at high tide and it's a beautiful sunny day.

I am grateful and I am gladly embracing it.

~ Cindy Bourgaize ~

The Open Door Way

When I am standing in front of the open doorway
The sun shines in ... let the sun in
Be the light ... share the light
Tap into the light ... my heart becomes the light
New opportunities, so grateful to be alive

When I stand in front of the open doorway
A new world of opportunities ... move on out
Be an example ...grabbing hands to tug others along
Lead the way ...don't look back
Feeling hope in new opportunities, so grateful to be alive

When I stood in front of the open doorway
Feeling peace, joy, love ...wanting to share the same
The past is the past ... no longer limited by it
Was shown the door when I needed it ...feeling free
Feeling new opportunities, so grateful to be alive

The open doorway ...
Gratitude for new opportunities ...the sun lights the way
No doubt about moving forward ... don't look back
Doing my best ...the best is good enough
So grateful to be alive

~ Norm Eygenraam ~

I AM

It was when she ventured out from under the veil of self-doubt that she finally was able to proclaim and embrace the life she had always dreamed of.

She had had enough of hiding just beneath the surface of the woman she knew she was meant to be.

She had grown tired of trying to fit in when all the while fitting in was the last thing she needed to do and she knew it.

Layer by layer she peeled it back to expose what had been cloaked for too many years.

She felt a wave of excitement releasing from her heart and find its way to her throat.

But this time instead of the knee jerk reaction to suppress it, she instead set it free, as tears of joy streamed down her cheeks, she bawled,

"I AM here, I AM here to stay!".

~ Cindy Bourgaize ~

Stone

I am like a stone,
powerful winds and rain,
an order of chaos,
manifest by the universe itself.
Is the universe of love?
 I am like a stone,
while my skin is scarred by time itself;
while some of my brothers crack and crumble, and turn to dust,
I have a hidden power,
Am I made of love?
I am like a stone.
Knowing my true self,
A lattice of elements; emerald,
Forged in a mountain,
Heat and time, slowly changing.
I am like a stone.
I grow, from a seed; such a small impurity.
Now, I am love, I am beautiful.
Am I like a stone?

~ Jeff Brush ~

Smell the Roses

The petals are wrapped up tight
Scared to release its blossom to the world
But with courage, one petal falls open
Then another
And another
Realizing they are a much more beautiful blossom
Fully open to the world
The rest follow suit
A beautiful rose sharing itself with the world
Stopping to sniff it every time I walk by
Through its openness, it brings a smile to me
Every time I connect with its beauty
United in love together
A simple flower raises the vibration
Of its tiny corner of the world
Stopping to smell the roses
And sharing the love with all that your energy can touch

~ Andrea Eygenraam ~

Freedom

Centered I am
Grounded I am
Here, Now
Free
Flowing
To life itself

Strong I am
Clear I am
Feet flat
Connected
From generations past
And generations to come

Eternity
Infinity
Endless
Boundless

A privilege of this human experience is
To express who I am
To share my inner processes
To identify my lessons
And to bring responsibility to me

To give meaning when there's no meaning
To make useful when there is neglect and injury
To allow compassion when there is vulnerability, you see

Centered I am
Grounded I am
For life flows freely
Towards life itself
A woman
As me
Here, now
Free

Free from doubts
Although doubts are awakening
Free from hesitations
Although hesitations are opportunities to get clear
Free from my thoughts
Although thoughts are informative
Free from my Selves
Although my Selves are the many facets of the human experience
Towards Me
Towards You
Towards Us
Free

~ Suzie Nunes ~

Just One More Thing....

In this world, in this thing called life, I like to think that each day we learn lessons and if we are fortunate enough to make it to perhaps becoming what is considered wise because you have some experience under your belt, life actually becomes less complicated. Less complicated because your perception changes.

So, each day I wake up and I try to remember to say two things:

First of all, thank you, thank you for another day

And second of all, what can I do today that will make the world a better place?

There are many diseases, hardships, injustices and sorrows, and there is compassion, beauty, appreciation and thankfully, love.

As far back as I can remember, I always felt as if I had to put forth extra effort to mentally, physically, emotionally measure up to the world's standards of what "normal" should be.

I had no idea that I had been born with Ulcerative Colitis, which affects you mentally, physically and emotionally, therefore always thought that I didn't measure up, I wasn't good enough because I didn't meet the standards of what a "normal" functioning human being was expected to be.

I pushed forward and took on an attitude that it was all about working hard, setting very high standards for myself and those around me, if you work hard enough you'll be successful.

I am here to tell you that that is wrong thinking.

That you need to listen to your heart, get quiet and hear your inner voice, love yourself for who you are, not what you think the world expects you to be.

Do what works for you.

We have but one life to live and I am telling you don't spend another minute looking outside yourself for answers.

Each and every life on this planet is valuable.

We have no idea what each individual has been through or is feeling at any given moment, or what their limit is.

At my worst is when I have learned the most valuable life lessons.

One day while visiting with Gran not long after my diagnosis in 2012 I told her about it. I knew she had endured years of suffering and pain and kept silent most all of the time.

She said "Do you think that it is better to know what it is?"

I wasn't sure how to respond. I wasn't sure what she was getting at.

I've mulled that over in my head from many angles.

What I do know is that it has always been with me, it's part of me, and it has gotten worse over the years.

I understand that it has taught me how to love and accept myself and others, taught me to change my focus, that it's ok to slow down take care of me before I've reached my absolute limit.

It's taught me to see others through a different lens.

That if "just one more thing" is added to my load, then that is when I need compassion, appreciation, beauty and love most.

So out there, in this world, in this thing called life, I try to remember when I see others, struggling, "just one more thing".

.

~ Cindy Bourgaize ~

Seasons of Change

Everything has a season.

Life is ever changing. It flows constantly – the winds scatter the leaves of time, the waters wash the sorrows down the river, the fires flame the hearts desires, the earth holds us steady with its slow and solid movement. Yet, our world is frantic; dramatic; full of pain and sorrow, confusion and delusion.

At what point do we wake up? At what point do we realize that change is the only constant in our lives? What would it feel like to embrace change? To truly go with the flow in all aspects of our world. Some might argue that our inner sanctum, our Spirit, never changes - so in reality change doesn't have to be a constant. Stillness, oneness, Joy, LOVE…they could be our constants. YES. And how would we get from the ever-present changes in the outer world, to the constant of Love from the inner world reflected outward?

Embrace the changes in your life. Allow the rivers to flow, the people to come and go, and the desires to grow and wane as new desires come about. Perhaps finding the stillness is more about recognizing the shifts, the changes…recognizing where we put our attention and deciding if that is bringing us more drama or more peace. How do we get there?

Today is a journey, a stepping stone to our inner most desire – this moment brings us the opportunity to choose and to choose again.

We are taught that everything has a season. The cycles of time show that to us. Watch Nature. Each season has a purpose. Each season brings new opportunities, presents life in a different state, and always flows from one to the next. Our life is like that. Our activities, the friends we have, the jobs we do, are all like that. Each has a season, each has a purpose and each will be fulfilled in the exact right way and right time. So, why do we live such frenetic lives? Why do we honour what others "expect" or "want" of us, only to ignore what is right and honouring in our own selves?

As beings on this Human Holiday, we have many beliefs that have taken hold to guide our travels. Much of the time we don't even recognize what drives or motivates us. We go through this holiday on automatic pilot, regurgitating old habits and other's way of thinking. We cling so strongly to traditions and the "way things have always been done", that we miss the essence and meaning behind the origin of the tradition. Traditions can be wonderful opportunities – they bring people together to share, to laugh, to love and to honour – they can be very powerful connections. Or they can turn out to be the added dimension to more stress and anxiety in our world. It is a matter of perspective.

Our belief system may shape the direction of our life, but it is our emotional guidance system that will remind us of our true journey to Self. When we pay attention to how we really, honestly, feel about a situation (a change in circumstances, a shift in relationship, a move to a new house…anything), we have an opportunity to embrace the beauty of the seasons of our life. We have the occasion to change our minds, to decide for ourselves where Peace lies and what we truly wish to choose for. The unknown is not to be feared, for if we never let go of what holds us down, we will not have the chance of reaching for what brings us up, brings us joy. Life is meant to be lived in Light; recognizing the shadow – the fears we may have, the stubbornness we may have created – allows us to open the shades a bit and see life from a new perspective.

Seasons are a wonderful thing. Change is a season. Embrace each season for what it has to offer and watch the flow of your own life become more of everything you desire. Realizing our Infinite Potential starts with recognizing that we are the directors, that we have the potential to BE and experience all that we desire. In this time of Thanksgiving, I give thanks for all the wonderful people who have been part of my life, past, present and future. I give thanks for knowing that each person brought a unique gift to my journey. Some may still be with me, others I may have let go of or lost contact with – but they are still valued. The joy comes in knowing that every season, every change, is a gift. As I continue to explore my Human Holiday – floating on a river of Peace – I encourage you to embrace whatever changes are happening in your life right now. Start recognizing the Infinite Potential of You!

~ Lisa D. Theodore ~

EARTH
Grounding Us as One in Spirit & Meditation

Priceless is Our Worth

All around the world there are places of delusion
Corners of the universe filled with confusion
A ribbon tying us in misery and despair
The human condition of thought takes us there
Then, when you clear the smoky haze
Turning your back on those places and days
You begin to see new corners in the world
Hope and possibility begins to unfurl
You realize there is another thread
A different way for your story to be read
Spirit takes over and to faith you surrender
A place in the world that is ours to render
As we waiver from each fold in our own time
We perceive the world as a place more kind
Seeking compassion instead of despair
Finding in people what was always there
A ribbon that binds us in understanding; and then
We feel more as one, united to defend;
Against falling into the chasm of misery and despair
It is easier now, though fear's always there;
To feel that others can identify
Not just on the surface, but deep and allied
All around the world we ebb and we flow
Like rivers, lakes and oceans on and on we will go
Natural and beautiful connected by the earth
Together bonded, making priceless our worth.

~ Lisa Colbert ~

Empowered Hearts

The flame burns bright inside me
I will not let it be extinguished
The fire in me ignites others
And together we burn away the toxins
Leaving only ashes after the embers die out
I will not fan them or try to ignite them again
I will watch them smolder and fade
I will rise with a stronger heart
Shining my light for all to see
A lighthouse guiding the way home
For any others willing to look for it
Open hearts letting in the light
Igniting each other and lifting all up
Rising higher than we ever have
Together we can light the world
One flame at a time becoming brighter
As we join together, stronger united
Love will not be conquered
It will spread like wildfyre
Community of love sharing, growing, learning
Lighting the way for all those willing
To dance in the flames

~ Andrea Eygenraam ~

You've Never Been Forgotten

Aloha!
Greeting this day
Seizing THE day
THE Present Moment
Of Our lives
And
Of Mindfulness

Courage for Being Ourselves
A True Being
Worthy
Simply because WE exist
In Oneness
With the Loving and Creative
Spirit
United as ONE

As WE are
Knowing and Seeing
Listening
Mindful and Aware
You've never been forgotten
Of what is there

Focused
Concentrated
Living deeply
The Moment
Of Every Breath
Of Every Step

Our Mind and Our Body
Aligned
In ONE direction
Together

Smile
Your beautiful Smile
Present
Before my Eyes
A True Gift
Where Life is Possible
Here
In this Present Moment

Touch my Heart
Found
Here
In this Present Moment

Here
And
Now

Where
LIFE
Lives
And
Has many Wonders
WonderFULLy
Filled
Timeless Awareness
Expanded through Gratitude
Spacious Gratitude
Soaked

And Incorporated
HEALING
And
WHOLE

Touch my Breathing
I know
I AM
Breathing IN
I know
I AM
Breathing OUT

Mind, Body, and Spirit
Come Together
In
Oneness
Back to Yourself
Present
In the Here
And
In the Now
EveryONE can BE
THAT

Available
To Love Yourself
And to Love The Other
Knowing there are still many elements
Of Peace, Love, Joy, and Happiness
Living within You

Mindfulness
IS
The Practice of Love

Nourishing First
Deeply
Touching First
Deeply
With
Peace

FooIn our Body, our Feelings and Our Consciousness
In Our World
Having the Power to Heal
Knowing
You Have Never Been Forgotten
Still playing the role
Of Peace and
Of Wellbeing for
US
Protecting Peace
Nourishing Peace
Growing Peace
WE ALL CAN

For You are Spirit
United
As ONE
Guided and Supported
Revealing Yourself
In Wholeness
Complete
Seeing
And
Touching
Deeply
Understanding
Compassion

Here
Now
Giving Peace a Chance
In EveryDay
ToDay
Seizing the Day
Greeting this Day
Aloha!

~ Suzie Nunes ~

Selfless

I opened the box in front of me and discovered that in my haste, I had grabbed the wrong box.

My heart sank with disappointment as I glumly gazed at some of my old clothing I had intended to give to goodwill for "someone in need". In the other box, a few of my favorite newer sweaters I was packing away for the upcoming winter.

At first, I was selfishly thinking only of myself and how I would go about retrieving my precious box of sweaters. I had dropped the box off that morning at one of those randomly placed goodwill bins you see in parking lots in any given town. I thought if I was really fortunate I would drive down and the box would still be there, untouched. I imagined the glee I would feel at being reunited with my cozy, comfy sweaters.

Suddenly I experienced a peculiar shift in my thinking, as I quite often do since my awakening and my discovery of self-love. I began to think about that "someone in need", that someone who may have had to settle for older clothing lately as a result of circumstances beyond her control. I envisioned this "someone in need" discovering the box of cozy, comfy sweaters. I visualized her face lighting up with delight and felt her heart expanding with joy.

Unselfishly, I decide that I would not be retrieving my box of cozy, comfy sweaters, but instead, I wanted "someone in need" to experience them and I happily send expanding love and magnificent light along with them.

~ Cindy Bourgaize ~

Footprints in Paradise

I felt the hair on my arms stand up.

Where am I? As I look around, I notice the whiteness of the sand, the cool breeze coming off the ocean and the vivid green of the palm trees and vegetation of the island.

I am not alone! I feel the presence of another being, but not of this lifetime.

He is a tall man, with long dark hair swirling about His ruggedly handsome face, sporting a beard. His eyes are piercing but the smile is what catches my attention!

Come walk with me, He gestures. As we make our way down the beach, I notice he is barefoot, just like I am.

We stroll along, in a comfortable silence, neither wanting to break the easy comfort between us.

What peace I feel, like this is where I've wanted to be my whole life. The colours of the trees, bright green, the foliage contrasting against the white sand, the striking blue of the ocean with the white caps formed by the breeze coming in.

This is my idea of paradise – a go-to place to ease my mind of the day to day interruptions of life, a place where no one can be, accept me and my "friend", and I can find a tranquility like nowhere else.

I love this place! I love my "friend"! And I love the way I feel when I am here!

I look behind me, and watch as the waves of water vanish the footprints we have made in the sand. Once there…then the next second gone.

Then I notice…sometimes there are only one set of footprints!
Who is this "friend" of mine? It can only be one being!
Now I know why I love this place!

~ Lorraine Phillips ~

Cycles Cycles

The cycle cycles,
Cycle to sprout,
Cycle to grow,
Cycle to thrive,
And to pass survive!
The beginning of a sprout,
Engorged and transformed, and
Ignited where there's no turning back!
Forever changing, moving.
Evolving and accepting,
Life as it unfolds before me.
I,
The observer.
You,
The observer.
Mirroring each other.

Becoming clear windows.

Be windows.

Clear windows.

With integrity

And truth.
We are one.
In Gratitude.

~ Suzie Nunes ~

Scintilla

I am but a scintilla in the Universe,
but the Universe revolves around me.
I am a part of all that is, and was and will be.
When I shift, everything shifts.
This is not ego - this is physics.
I watched as a hologram of my DNA double helix appeared in my vision.
It rotated and changed before my eyes.
The colours of the rainbow were vividly shining
from different aspects of it.
My conscious mind I sensed is unaware of what is happening,
but my spirit is making the changes for me as I grow and evolve.
I know I'm on the precipice of something huge
and I have no fear of that – only curiousity and anticipation.
I am Love.

~ Elaine Hutchinson ~

Dropping into the Zone

Dropping into the zone - the infinite stream of wisdom, truth and understanding of the highest.
All the information you ever need, are ever searching for flows through this infinite, everlasting stream.
A consciousness beyond time, beyond self - an energy, a vibration so purely vibrant and brilliant words can never adequately convey the vastness of this flow.
Running in, through, around all that is. Dropping into the zone, the Tao, the All that is - our "God" space - a moment of silence and we are there and everywhere all at the same time.
A moment of intention and the path illuminates.
A moment of reflection and all is apparent.
The still, quiet voice of the Infinite lands quietly in our mind; droplets of loving support guiding us along our journey.

Dropping into the zone - finding the expansiveness within; reaching our Divine creation, ourselves.

Dropping into the zone - dipping into the Cosmic understanding of our own deepest desires; popping back up like a bobber in the water floating atop the ocean of life.

Dropping into the zone - refreshing & recharging; cool, crisp, clear.

Dropping into the zone - allowing the flow of all that there is to gently move past; reflections shining up to you as your thoughts take you along the current.
What is your desire, your focus; where do you want to go; how do you want to BE?
Letting go of the struggle; floating on the waves of consciousness - lightness, brightness - intense joy and love pouring through each cell as it drinks from the well of All that Is.

Following the true nature of our heart as we drop further into the void, the emptiness...the zone.
Realizing the potential of all things as we recognize the void is really the All.
Realizing anything is possible.
The Universe holds the space of the Truth, the wisdom of all of our Being.
Everything we can dream - we can see - we can be.
We have the support of the Infinite, the Tao; the way which illuminates our soul, guiding us through the zone and back again with all the resources we need for our ride through this lifetime and eternity. ....
As we speak of one, we speak of all.
The I becomes the We.
The solitary journey becomes the travels of everyone and everything.
The separation fades; vision opens.
The pictures turn to feelings, a sense of knowingness, a sense of truth.
A what Is, IS moment where the illusion of uniqueness and separation falls away.
There is one flow, one Love vibration, and it moves through all creation and time.
We, You, I are all connected in this continuum.
Our intention and focus bring to light that which we wish to see, to embrace, to manifest and to create.
Our deepest moments of regret turning into our greatest joys.
Expanding through this limiting vision and belief of this moment into the infinite Divine potential that awaits - the Source - the bubbling effervescence of unconditional Love, Truth, Wisdom and Understanding awaits.
In the distractions of this world, the Infinite still resides.
In the frenzy and frantic moments of this world - where molecules bang around creating a seeming cacophony of distraction, annoyances, worries, road blocks - the zone holds the space to return to our infinite potential.
The Universe is ever ready to respond to our call - our intention and thoughts guiding our way along the superhighway of Love.

Where do you want to travel?
How do you choose to move through each day - tapping into the ease and grace of the Universal flow; or caught in the whirlwind of false belief and attachment to pain and suffering.
Allow for just a moment, a few seconds, to drop into the zone to hang out in your heart space and connect with the incredible vibration of All that Is - You. Come Play.

~ Lisa D. Theodore ~

You Are Not Alone

There was a flower that stood alone
in a valley surrounded by fields of mountain flowers.
One day, as it was feeling particularly lonely
it asked God, "Why do you have me standing alone?"

God replied,
"The other flowers do not have your purpose little one.
They need each other to hold them up from day to day.
You, My little one, stand alone
because my plans for you are far greater.

If I had put you among the others
you would not have had the nutrients from My soil
to give you the strength you will need.
You would not have had the water from My rain
that was needed to purify you.

And if the others stood too tall beside you
you would not have received the sun you need
to grow in My Light.

I have great plans for you, my little one
know that you are never alone.
My Light shines in you
and if you trust in Me
My Light will shine through you
When I need it to."

~ Susan Garand ~

Fire Passion Meditation

This meditation is to fill your hearts with passion so you may take it with you in any situation whether that be with your partner, an art project or just simply writing in your journals. You are going to be waking the fire energy within you to kick start your passion. You are going to pull the energy right up from the fiery center of mother earth.

When we are done you will feel this connection to yourself and to the energy from above and below that will fill your heart and soul.
You will own your own passion.
Close your eyes.
Take a deep breath.
Take another.

Imagine a white light coming down on top of your head. This light is coming from the energies above.
The white light starts to surround your head, starting with the crown chakra. Letting this light in you start to feel it as it comes down to your eyes.
Now your face
All the way around the back of your head.
It's now starts to come down your neck.
See this light coming down to your chest.
Around your back and spine, straightening you up.
Now down your arms.
Feel it all around your torso.
Feel as it comes into your sacred chakra.
Now your root chakra.
Feel the light inside your whole body.

See it coming down to your thighs and legs. Down to the souls of your feet.
The white light is now ready to enter the earth.
Coming from your feet it is now connecting you from the universe above to the earth below.
The white light continues going down though the ground below your feet, all the way passing the many layers of dirt, rock and sand.

Penetrating the earth's crusts.
All the way down to the hot lava of the center of this great creation.
You are now connected from the universe above all the way to the center of the earth.
Feel the fiery lava connecting to the white light.
The heat starting to rise up knowing that this will not burn you let the heat rise.
.
.
.

It is now at your feet moving slowly up though each of your 7 chakras one by one.
You're Root Chakra
Sacral Chakra
You feel the passion start to rise in you.
Your Solar plexus chakra
Now your heart chakra from there your
Throat chakra
And third eye chakra
It moves all the way up to your crown chakra and goes through it.
Now the passion from the fiery lava is connected to the energy above.
How does this make you feel?
.
.
.

The passion from the fire starts to come down around you. It is creating a fire Sphere all around you.
No one can touch you in your fire Sphere.
Remember it cannot hurt you.
You are now surrounded with this wonderful sense of passion.
You can do anything you wish.
Enjoy the feeling of this passion you have just unlocked. Use it. Let it serve you.

Start to count to 5.
Start to bring your awareness back.
1
2
Start to feel your body again. Move your fingers and toes.
3
4
Your almost totally back
5
Now open your eyes.
Write how this made you feel. The passion that is now inside of you and all around you. What feelings does this bring up?
Blessed be

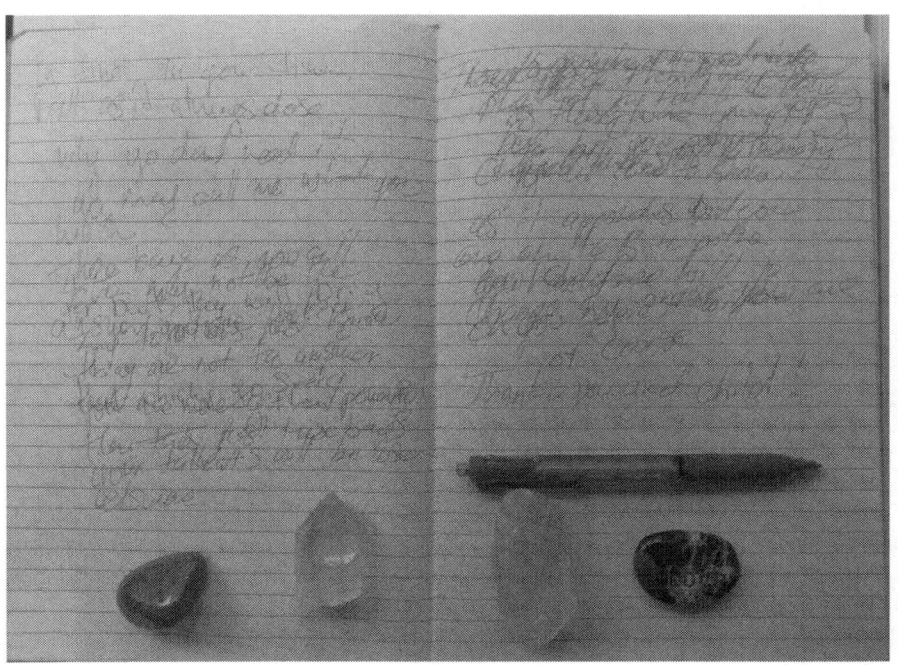

~ Lisa Snow ~

Fire Ceremony Meditation

This meditation was channeled by the goddess Danu.
Start by sitting down, if with a group please sit in a circle and hold hands.

Say "I am setting the intention of spiritual growth"
We are all here to do this together and to connect with our sisters.
As we sit here now holding hands I ask that you all take a deep breath in and feel the support of your sisters sitting next to you.
Feel the strength and firmness of their grip. They are holding you as tight as you are holding them.
Release your hands.

I ask that you make yourself comfortable and when you are ready close your eyes.
We are going on a journey with each other.

Take a deep breath in. (if you are reading breathe along with them)
We will do this 3 times total.
On the 3rd exhale go deep and release any ill will that you have been carrying around with you.
This could be any stress from family, work or just daily struggles.
Now in your mind, you are in a circle of sisters. These can be of your life now or past. Know that these women are here to lead us.
Each goddess here now including yourself is very gifted and loved.
Feel the love from all around.

Now in your mind imagine all your sisters are holding hands as you were all before but this time with those sisters from now and past.
As you are all now holding hands start to walk around in a circle, you are all now moving around a giant fire in the middle of this amazing circle of strong women.

As you walk around the circle the speed starts to pick up.
You become more relaxed you start to move even faster.
Release your hands now as your walk starts to turn into a dance.
Feel yourself whooshing and swirling around the fire like you are the only one around.

Feel the energy of those around you, feel how alive you are!
Notice how free you are!
Dance now to the rhythm that is playing in your heart.
Keep moving.
You are now the only person standing in front of the fire.
Stare into it, what do you see?

.

.

.

Know you are safe and protected by your sisters.

.

.

.

Now sit in front of the fire and stare at it until it starts to burn out.

.

.

.

As the fire starts to turn into smoke, imagine all your fears and insecurities are going up in smoke with it.
You are now leaving behind all those feelings as you are supported by new and more positive feelings of love and connection to all those that stand with you.

.

As you sit, feel the air brush your skin.
Feel the earth beneath you.
Now touch the earth around you and imagine you are being rooted and becoming one. Know you are part of mother earth and so are your sisters.
know you are supported.
As you are all now grounded I ask that you start to come back to this energy plane, slowly.
Take your time.
Start to notice your breath again.
Take 3 deep breaths, as we did when we started.

.

Start to move your toes and fingers.
Move around in your spot and when you are ready you may open your eyes and see the world as new.
Blessed be.
~ Lisa Snow ~

Self-Love Meditation

This meditation is meant to close off the book in a peaceful loving way to honour yourself. It is also available online if that is easier for you to follow along. You've been through a journey sharing this book with us, make sure to honour yourself.

When you are ready, find a comfortable spot in your chair, and close your eyes, hands resting softly in your lap or at your sides.
Bring your attention to your breath.
Inhale a deep cleansing breath into the bottom of your lungs and into your belly, letting it expand.
And now, softly let it go, let it go
Connect to the feeling of your breath inside you. Feel as your belly rises on the breath in and releases as you breathe out. Embrace this rhythm
Take a couple more breaths until you feel fully connected to the rhythm of your breath
Breathe in again, imagining white light filling up inside you cleansing and energizing you.
Breathe out slowly, slowly, letting your exhaling breath softly taking with it any thoughts weighing you down from the day.
Breathe in again, letting the white light fill up every corner in your body, deeper, deeper.
Now when you breathe out, let your breath take with it any remaining stress that may be left inside you, softly, slowly.
Bring your attention to your feet flat on the ground. Imagine you're like a tree, with red glowing roots coming down your legs and out of your feet and going down through the building and further down still into the soil and down down into the core of the earth, connecting you with mother nature. Her power is yours to draw from and you feel that energy surging through your body.
Tense up your toes and release them, and slowly move up to your calves and your thighs, tensing each muscle group and holding it for a moment and then releasing. Feel the muscles tense up under you in your chair and let them go. Now straighten your back arching your shoulders back and roll them forward to let it go.

Tense up your hands and fingers, and shake them out to release it. Feel the muscles in your neck and back of the head release as you let them go and feel lighter. Squish up your face muscles for a final release and stretch your jaw to let all the stress and tension go. Imagine a green spinning ball of energy in the middle of your chest filling you up with warmth and love and light, expanding as you become more aware of it.

See in your mind's eye, that glowing white light you breathed in, flowing out the top of your head and connecting you with the universe around you, expanding all the way up to the moon and further further beyond as your relaxation grows.

You are feeling more open and receiving all the energy of the universe that is there for you. Rest in this feeling of connectedness for a moment.

Feeling this connection to everything around you, picture in your minds eye, your favourite place, the place when you need a break from your every day life, where you go to feel safe. It can be real or imagined, but get a picture of it in your mind. What does your place look like? How do you feel when you are safe in your place? Are there any special sounds unique only to your place? Maybe it's a smell that takes you back and reminds you of this place of comfort. Go deeper into visualizing this place, deeper, deeper, wrap yourself in that feeling of security and love. Feel it all around you, calming you, relaxing you. Rest in this space you have accessed in your mind. Open your heart to the whole experience, letting go of the outside world. Feel that there is a space in your heart of all that you have let go of tonight and throughout this year. Feel that void, knowing there's room for so much more than you are even aware of, and anything is possible as you move forward into this coming year with hope and love.

Imagine now, that there's a bucket in front of you and it has your name on it. Study your bucket and become familiar with it. Is it a steel bucket or maybe plastic? Maybe it's a wooden barrel type. Is your name engraved or painted on? Imagine gripping the sturdy handle, you feel how secure your bucket is.

Beside it now, you see some words. Fun, Silly, Creative, Adventurous, Resourceful, Strong...Take one of these words and put it in your bucket. Kind, Generous, Courageous...Now place another in there. Loving, Caring, Happy...Keep filling your bucket with words that you feel describe you and any other words that you see around you.

Now you see another set of words, self care, self esteem, relaxation, assertiveness. Place some of these into the bucket too of what you'd like more of. Patient, Healthy, Accepting.

As you look at your bucket that's nearly full now, feel your body filled with love for all that you are and are working to become. Pick it up and feel the weight of the words and how secure they are in your bucket.

Know that the bucket is yours and yours alone. Those words are all possible, and fill your heart with hope and love. Sit with your bucket for a moment and let yourself absorb everything that you put in it. One last deep breath into this relaxation and completeness, feeling one with your soul's desires.

You are leaving this place for now, but you can come back to your favourite place anytime you feel you need to. Just take yourself back with your breath. It's your favourite safe place, and your bucket will be here waiting as a reminder to you.

Now gently start coming back to the present room, feeling yourself settle into your entire body, becoming more grounded, more present, more aware with my every word. Feel yourself in the chair, feel the air on your skin, feet firmly on the ground, coming back only when you are fully ready. When you're ready, wiggle your toes and wiggle your fingers, cover your eyes as you blink them open to gently adjust and do a few stretches and shake off anything left inside.

Thank you for coming to sit with us on this journey

Photo Credits, with Gratitude

12 – Cindy Bourgaize
27, 52, 136, 156 – Lisa D. Theodore
32, 40, 57 – Suzie Nunes
35, 110 – Norm Eygenraam
45, 73 – Andrea Beaver Dennis
11, 29, 43, 51, 69, 77, 91, 103, 104, 117, 125, 139, 163 – Andrea Eygenraam

INDEX

Abdulkarim Farah	36
Andrea Beaver Dennis	54,62,69,71,122
Andrea Eygenraam	38,74,101,108,115,131,141,160
Cindy Bourgaize	12,14,15,25,126,129,134,146
Diane O. Taylor	35,37,45,49,55,119,119
Elaine Hutchinson	149
Elena Pastura	30,100
Heather Embree	66
Jeff Brush	130
Jeff Martin	72,121,123
Jenny Kuspira	13,16,20,56,59,80,84,118
Jessica Schuler-Feng	17,19,21,78,104,114,120
Jodi Cronyn	89,92
Keith Withers	107
Lorraine (Lainy) Phillips	147
Lisa Colbert	58,60,70,111,113,140
Lisa Snow	153,157
Lisa D. Theodore	26,52,136,150
Norm Eygenraam	128
Pamela Simmonds	18,22,42,46,82,90,109
Rebecca Lofsnes	63
Sarah Farr	44,64,112
Susan Garand	34,39,152
Suzie Nunes	32,40,65,68,132,142,148
Tammy Arbour	24
Valerie Malcovich	73

The Awesome Authors in this Book

My name is Abdulkarum Farah. I was born in Kismayo, Somalia in 1981. I came to Canada in 1990 and have lived here ever since. I am a fan of poetry and freestyle rap as well as the arts in general. Thank you and God bless!

Andrea Beaver Dennis resides in Guelph and is a proud mother. She is building a new spiritual business being a guiding lighthouse for those who seek it. You can find Guided by Light on facebook and email her at stardust62@gmail.com

Cindy Bourgaize was born amidst the grandeur of the ocean and mountains in the picturesque town of Gaspe, Quebec, her first love. She is passionate about being one with Mother nature. Cindy believes that simplicity is beauty and considers herself a budding minimalist. She currently resides in Cambridge, Ontario.

Diane O. Taylor is an artist attending Laurier University. She has been creatively writing since an early age, publishing many articles and photos on through university. Currently Diane is working on a self-reflective piece and continues to try her creative hand at many different genres.

Elaine Hutchinson is semi-retired and currently resides in Grimsby, ON. She is a Reiki Master, Metamorphic Practitioner and intuitive healer on the spiritual path. She enjoys the inspired free-fall style of writing the Guided Pen offers. Elaine never knows where the story will go, and often gets surprising insight.

Elena Pastura was born in Italy and moved to Toronto in 1993, where she taught. In 2011 she moved to Stratford, where she successfully runs Birmingham Manor Bed and Breakfast. Her many interests include baking, cooking theatre, photography, gardening, travelling and reading. Lately she has been exploring her creativity with felting and writing.

Heather Embree is a children's author, poet and freelance writer in Guelph, ON. She is also a professional intuitive and medium, supporting the caring hearts who need healing in a hurting world. She is also a proud Child-free Woman, which has allowed her to write, travel, learn Spanish, relate with many people and be actively involved in the community. She loves Zumba, artists, alternative healing, and meditating. You can find out more about her at: www.blossomingheart.ca

Hello, my name is Jeff Brush, I am a musician, a father of two amazing boys, and am dating an remarkable woman who is an even more pheonomenal author. I love all things guitar related, science fiction, cooking and life in general. I have future plans for my low-fi brush audio channel @ YouTube, including original music, guitar pedal/equipment reviews, and more; I can be emailed at **brushaudiomodifications@gmail.com** for all inquiries.

My name is Jeff Martin and was born in Canada. In my 43 years I have lived in Costa Rica for 5 years. I am a Spiritual being who strives to grow and learn every day. I was involved in a very serious motorcycle accident about 25 years ago resulting in a traumatic brain injury, paralysis of my left arm and eventual amputation. My past has dictated my experiences but I, through my word and integrity, create who I am today and every day anew! I love to inspire others: species, volunteering or organizing fund raisers. I am a vibrant life force of energy and love to create every day. My web site is: www.inspirationcorer.ca

Jennifer J. Kuspira loves life! Her work and passion are about inspiring others to be their best; whether it is at her Full-time work as a Developmental Services Worker, an Educational Assistant, or as an Independent Brand Partner with Nerium international. Jenny also motivates others through her writing, and involvement with the Guelph Guild of Storytellers.
J.J.Kuspira@gmail.com
Jennyqh.nerium.com

Jessica Schuler-Feng is a teacher working in a private international high school in Mississauga, Ontario. Originally from Stoney Creek, she spent many years living abroad in Guangzhou, China teaching ESL and other subjects. It was there where she discovered her true passion for travel and adventure, and also met her wonderful husband! If you want to learn more about her or about her writing, please feel free to reach out to her at jschuler_sdhs@yahoo.ca

A tantrika is defined as a woman who isn't defined by anything, living compassionately, lovingly, blissfully, and fearlessly, and that is what Jodi Cronyn aims to embody. A yogi, wellness enthusiast, world traveller, and soul seeker, her love of writing and expression developed at a young age, and she has since gone on to share her work through her blog and social media. Her community is called Wild Fyre, and their slogan is #findyourfyre, for passion is everything she stands for in life, encouraging people to live more from the heart, and less from the mind. Dreams are always worth seeking. Adventures are always worth having. A heart is always worth loving. Peace, always.
www.wildfyre.ca Facebook: @wildfyre11 Instagram @wild__fyre @thesaltyogi @wildfyreretreats

Keith comes from Stoney Creek, Ontario. Stung by the written word bug when he was in high school, he started writing screenplays and other treatments after. A lover of puns and wordplays. Also a follower of the saying "Don't Forget to Be Awesome"

Lorraine (Lainy) Phillips is a payroll associate with 40+ years of experience. She currently resides in Grimsby, Ontario. She loves to read, write, and do many kinds of crafts. The Guided Pen started her on her writing path when it showed her the freedom that free fall writing promises. She is also a Reiki Master, has her Energy Practitioner certification, and currently is head healer at her Spiritualist Church. Oh yes, and in the spring of 2019, she will become a Spiritualist Minister.

Lisa Snow lives in Cambridge ON with her husband Jay. She has been able to connect with spirit since the age of 1 when she crossed over briefly. Lisa is the creator of Sacred Snowflake Medium and not only helps the living but the dead as well. Follow her on social media @SacredSnowflakeMedium

Lisa D. Theodore, Min., RTCMP is a healer, educator & Spiritual Coach. She is the founder of The Qi Way: A Sanctuary for Alchemical Transformation, Healing & Education where she maintains a private clinical practice and educational space. Lisa offers classes in Qi Gong, Energy Medicine, & Healing arts. www.theqiway.com

Lisa Colbert is a talented writer with a natural spiritual flow. She is a Public Speaker and Workshop Facilitator. Lisa has shared her poetry in many public readings including Hamilton's Recovery Awareness Day events. She is especially passionate about the workshop she created called the Guided Pen, where meditation meets free fall writing to create a cathartic energy that brings self-discovery and healing. You can reach her @ vitalsparkca or her website at www.lisacolbert.ca

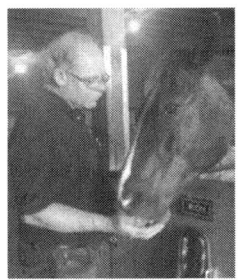

I am Norm and I have a small manufacturing business in Palmerston, Ontario. The spiritual journey which I have been on has been full of surprises with many twists and turns. I am now able to be more of a blessing to others and they to me as all of the "dots" are connecting and making more sense.

Pamela writes from a quintastic perspective about her life experiences as a woman over 50 at her website **www.aquintasticperspective.ca** . She divides her writing time between blogging, developing fictional stories and writing a collection of memoir essays describing her colourful and often challenging life.

Rebecca Lofsnes resides in lovely Downtown Kitchener. Mother to two teenage boys, she's also a very passionate yogini guiding yoga practitioners of all ages and levels with her business Flow State Yoga. A brain health advocate and ambassador for Allysian Sciences, she truly leads a life of health and wellness for the mind, body and spirit.

Sarah was first inspired to write by the poetic charm of folk singer, Billy Bragg. She began penning poetry which by fluke was accepted into a UK-published book of poems. Moving to Australia in her twenties, she settled in Canada after scratching a seven-year itch and rediscovered her love of writing.

SUZIE NUNES is a lover of life and a contemplator of the human experience and the love-consciousness in its perfection. She practices meditation, qigong, and plays crystal singing bowls for healing and for living more deeply in the awareness of love within her and the world. Born in Montreal, Quebec, and having travelled extensively the world, she now lives in Kitchener, Ontario since 2010. www.qigongoasis.com

After near death, I returned from heaven knowing things I had no way of knowing. Visions, prophesies, and Mediumship followed. Now, my sessions and my writing are guided by spirit and the angels. Find out more in my books, "FINDING MY WAY, An Assignment of Truth", and "LIFE'S GARDEN". Contact: **creator@creatorspen.com** or 1-855-GODS PEN (463-7736)

My name is Tammy Arbour and I am a proud wife and mother of two. I grew up in Northern Quebec in a large French & Irish family. After the sudden passing of my only daughter Alyshia (Rosie), I searched for signs of hope to keep me going. This poem is one of many hopeful moments she gifted me. It gave me oxygen and joy. I am grateful to able to share it with you all.

Always an avid reader, Valerie Malcovich is now discovering her writing skills. She belongs to both the reading and writing clubs at the public library. Valerie attended the Guided Pen classes and really enjoyed the inspired writing experience after the meditation ended. Valerie lives and loves Hamilton as her home.

Andrea Eygenraam is an Author, Speaker and Personal Development & Writing Coach, living in Stratford, ON with her border collie, tabby cat and creative partner. She helps people heal through creativity and live an inspired life. She runs workshops and does one on one coaching, combining metaphysical and traditional approaches to help people feel important and live their best life. She has wanted to be a published author since she was 3 years old, and now is living her dream, as well as helping others discover theirs. It really is possible to live your dreams, and she can help show you how. To find out more, visit MyInspiredCommunications.com or email andrea@myinspiredcommunications.com

Empowered Hearts is a product of connecting creative people through their words, love and healing, along with the desire to help others express themselves and build self-esteem.

Our words always sound better when spoken from the heart and shared, as many brave authors have done in this book. We hope you will keep on creating as well <3

If you're struggling, open a book and point to a sentence and use that as your starting line, or grab your copy of Busting Through Blocks, a soon to be released daily writing prompt book by Andrea Eygenraam, and get in a daily writing habit. Use the starting line/prompt to write without thinking for 10 or 15 minutes, even 5 minutes if that's all you have. Turn off the editor and don't worry about grammar or spelling. Give yourself that creative time and space and develop a daily writing habit and you will be surprised what you can create from your heart! There are guided meditations on Soundcloud and YouTube to help you get in the writing space (you can search Andrea Eygenraam as well) and then use your prompt and connect with your soul. It's worked to help hundreds heal, and it can work for you as well. If you feel compelled to share, email Andrea at **andrea@myinspiredcommunications.com** and maybe you will end up in our next book! 😊

Made in the USA
Columbia, SC
23 December 2017